WAGNER IN EXILE

RICHARD WAGNER IN 1862
Reproduced from the portrait by Cæsar Willich, painted from life
at Biebrich in 1862.

Historical Museum, Leipzig

WAGNER IN EXILE
1849–62

BY

WOLDEMAR LIPPERT
KEEPER OF THE PRINCIPAL PUBLIC ARCHIVES
OF SAXONY

TRANSLATED BY

PAUL ENGLAND

WITH HITHERTO UNPUBLISHED LETTERS AND
DOCUMENTS AND SIXTEEN ILLUSTRATIONS

GEORGE G. HARRAP & CO. LTD.
LONDON   BOMBAY   SYDNEY

First published 1930
by GEORGE G. HARRAP & CO. LTD.
39-41 *Parker Street, Kingsway, London, W.C.*2

Printed in Great Britain by Neill & Co. Ltd., Edinburgh

TO

MY WIFE

THE FAITHFUL PARTNER OF MY
JOYS AND SORROWS

PREFACE

AROUND the name of Richard Wagner, as is commonly the case with all great names, there has grown up a vast amount of literature dealing with every aspect of his life and works. Besides the complete biographies, we have books on special periods and events, books on his philosophy of life, on the man himself as poet, musician, friend, lover, revolutionary, and so on, to say nothing of his own writings and correspondence, and a mass of miscellaneous information.

The only justification for the present volume is the recent discovery of fresh material which enables me to throw new light upon a period of Wagner's existence that had a profound influence on the whole of his career. I refer to the years of his banishment—though banishment it was not at first, in the true sense of the word, but rather a voluntary exodus from his native land. Inevitably connected with this subject are the efforts made to procure his readmission into Germany, a step which Wagner regarded as indispensable to the further development of his musical career; and so we enter upon a long and fluctuating campaign of struggles, petitions, and pressure brought to bear in order to secure that official pardon on which his return depended.

Some of the facts are, of course, to be found in the

existing biographies and collections of letters, and a few of Wagner's petitions have been published; of these, however, some are given in the original draft, which differs considerably from the form finally adopted, while others are incomplete and mutilated, or misleading owing to their ascription to the wrong addressees (see Tille's valuable article on the Grand Duke Charles Alexander of Weimar *). The greater part of the evidence, however, has never yet been brought to light—even a specialist like Glasenapp could deny the existence of Wagner's first petition. In order to obtain the required material it was necessary to search the archives of the Saxon Ministry of Justice, the police papers in the Home Office, and the diplomatic documents in the Ministry for Foreign Affairs, besides the correspondence in the private archives of the King of Saxony. Lastly, I have gathered much valuable information from the Vienna archives (family, Court, and State), the Grand Ducal archives in Karlsruhe, the archives of the General Theatrical Management in Dresden, as well as from documents in the possession of private persons.

In accordance with Houston Chamberlain's contention that "Wagner's writings, with his letters and his works, will always be the most important, I might more properly say the *only* source from which we shall be able to derive a deeper knowledge of this extraordinary man." I have endeavoured to trace the ever-varying currents of his ideas in his own words. The ties that bound him to Germany and German art, the desire for restoration to his native land—these are

* For particulars see the " List of Principal Authorities " (p. 207).

8

the clues to his conduct throughout all the vicissitudes of those thirteen years. In quoting from his voluminous correspondence I have naturally not troubled to extract every trifling reference to the subject of his return, but have merely related the main incidents in his own language.

In the case of Wagner words and actions often seem so contradictory that we should be puzzled how to reconcile them were we to consider them independently. He writes to Mathilde Wesendonk in 1859, " I am certainly the maddest creature imaginable—and that is precisely the reason why I am a poet and—what is still worse—a musician." It is only when one examines his utterances in order and with regard to the events and conditions of the time that the riddle is solved, the tangled skein unravelled. It seemed best, then, to have recourse to the testimony of contemporary witnesses in order to show how the joyous sense of freedom with which Wagner entered on his exile soon gave place to a load of cares—how, little by little, the Master came to realize that even a creative genius can never free himself altogether from earthly ties, that while the poet may perhaps from time to time escape from the world around him, the composer is hampered even in his highest flights if deprived of those executive forces which alone enable him to make the creations of his genius live. I may add that, apart from the main subject of the book, my researches have enabled me to throw new and important light on many single episodes in Wagner's life during the period dealt with. From the abundant illustrations available of persons and places associated with Wagner at this time we have chosen such as are little known, or not known at all.

In conclusion I offer my heartiest thanks to the many custodians of archives, directors of museums, libraries, theatres, etc., who have kindly given me their valuable assistance.

W. LIPPERT

Niederlössnitz
Near Dresden

CONTENTS

ILLUSTRATIONS

NOTE

THE matter connected with the small reference numbers occurring in the text will be found in the section of Notes at the end of the book (pp. 191–205).

WAGNER IN EXILE

I

RICHARD WAGNER AND THE MAY REVOLUTION

1849-53

The Saxon Revolt—Settling in Zürich—Sense of
Newly Acquired Freedom.

OF all the events in Richard Wagner's lifetime the
one that was most pregnant with consequences
for him was the May revolution in Dresden in the
year 1849. In the many separate accounts of this event,
as well as in the larger biographies and in works concerned with other aspects of the affair, Wagner's share
in the stormy happenings of those days has been dealt
with more or less thoroughly, so that there is no need
to reopen the whole question again; certain details, it
is true, still await confirmation, but any fresh discoveries
are hardly to be expected—at least, so far as the official
records are concerned.

Richard Wagner in the character of a revolutionary
is certainly so odd a figure that one never tires of con-
templating it, especially as his participation in such
matters had the strongest possible influence on the
course of his life, and consequently on the activities
and output of the artist. Properly speaking it would
be paradoxical to class Wagner with the revolutionaries, since such men as a rule take naturally to politics,
either deliberately or through impulse, while Wagner

was by nature as little of a politician as it was possible for an educated person of that time to be; his incidental appearance on the political stage, awkward, unfortunate, amateurish, as it were, served merely to accentuate his utter unfitness for such a *rôle*. But in a nature so peculiar as Wagner's, so flighty, so changeable, passing so rapidly from one extreme to another, it is just this element of the contradictory, the unexpected, that we recognize as characteristic.

In no other way can we explain how a man who gratefully acknowledged the kindness he had received from King Frederick Augustus II, whom he regarded with almost extravagant reverence, could be betrayed into deeds and utterances that are in direct contrast to such an attitude. The truth is that Wagner was a sentimentalist through and through; so completely was he under the sway of his feelings that in every crisis of his existence they were powerful enough to exclude, or at least to paralyse for the time, the promptings of common sense. In one sense this exuberant emotionalism was Wagner's most valuable possession; it made it possible for him, even in his darkest hours, despite the crushing burden of material anxieties, to produce his mighty masterpieces, first in the form of poetry, and later to wed them to the loftiest music. Yet this same emotionalism it was that drove him to adventure on such tumultuous seas that more than once destruction seemed inevitable, and he was tempted to despair of himself, his art, his very existence.

The few sidelights we have to throw on his political performances will not detain us long. When in March 1848 Frederick Augustus II received the homage of his people after appointing the Liberal Braun-Georgi Ministry, Wagner, according to his own vivid description, was especially zealous in urging the people to acclaim their King with ever warmer demonstrations of joy and loyalty. Greatly excited, he ran with the crowd in order to arrive in time at the exact place where it seemed to him that " a particularly hearty greeting would rejoice and gratify the sovereign's heart." In his enthusiasm he shouted himself hoarse, and returned home in such a state of exhaustion that poor Minna was greatly alarmed.[1]

We have a priceless instance of his political muddle-headedness in his famous — or infamous — speech delivered on June 14 of the same year to the Vaterlandsverein, a society whose duty, according to him, was to exalt the democratic principle to the highest place and use the constitutional monarch merely as a necessary figurehead. Wagner's ideas can only be described as Utopian—impossible and utterly incompatible with any contemporary conception of the monarchy. In his fanatical idealism he assumes that every one else is prepared to accept his solution of the problem of how to escape from sober reality. He says:[2]

> We may surely demand that the King shall be the first and most thoroughgoing republican of all. Is not the King called, above all other men, to set the example of a good republican? Republic—*res publica*—means the public interest; what individual can be better suited than the King to devote himself with heart and mind and energy exclusively to the public interest?

Most of the reigning princes, it is true, seemed to him to fall far short of this ideal. He says of them:

> A blind, degenerate race, unfit for any lofty position.

With what sorrow do we gaze around on the German kingdoms—Hanover, Hesse, Bavaria—but why go further ? . . . We close our eyes to such a painful scene, but open them again upon our own dear country. Here we see the Prince whom his people love with genuine personal affection ; here is the man raised up by Providence ! Filled with such thoughts, I dare to say boldly and with enthusiasm, " We are republicans. Thanks to the march of progress, we are within reach of having a republic of our own." Alas, that word, we know, is still associated with every kind of fraud and wickedness—but all that might be ended by one word from our Sovereign ! It is not for us to proclaim the Republic—no ! But let our Prince, the noblest, worthiest of monarchs, speak the words, " I declare Saxony to be a Free State."

The first law of the Free State must be one which affords the fullest security for its existence : the highest executive power shall be in the hands of the Royal House of Wettin, and shall descend regularly by hereditary succession. So the King, as the head of the Free State, will be all that a king, in the noblest sense of the word, should be—the first of his people, the freest of the free ! And would not this be the best German interpretation of that saying of Christ's, " He that is greatest among you shall be your servant " ?

There could be no question of a general petition :

One signature only would be of valid authority in this connexion—that of our beloved Sovereign, for whom we ardently desire a fairer lot, an even happier position, than that which he now enjoys.

Such ideas as these could only offend all parties ; out-and-out republicans [1] would have nothing to do with such a monstrous travesty of a Free State as they deemed this to be, while to the honest citizens, as well as to Court and military circles, such utterances seemed to verge on the grotesque, and could not fail to make a painful impression. We do not know how they were

WAGNER'S ROOMS IN THE MARCOLINI PALACE

A view of the garden front of the Marcolini Palace (now the City Hospital) in the Friedrichstrasse in Dresden-Friedrichstadt. Wagner's study and music-room were in the second story (now No. 84).

received by the King, for whose ears they were mainly intended. He was probably more capable than anyone else of detecting the good intention, the honest endeavour that strove for expression in these tangled phrases ; though he might shake his head over them, he knew better than to treat them as a political offence. So much we may assume from his refusal, in spite of strong pressure, to take proceedings in the matter ; indeed, Wagner himself testifies to the King's kindly forbearance. No unfavourable criticisms, however, could bring Wagner to reason : he went calmly on his perilous way.

In the article " Deutschland und seine Fürsten " * which appeared in Röckel's *Sächsische Volksblätter* for October 15, 1848, and was attributed to Wagner, there is no longer that cordial desire to differentiate between the King of Saxony and his brother-rulers which we find in the June oration, while the article " Die Revolution" (April 8, 1849) is a lyrical outburst in praise of that

sublime goddess. See where she comes careering on the wings of the storm ! The lightning plays round her majestic brow ; in her right hand she holds a sword, and in her left a torch. Her vengeful eye is dark and cold— and yet what fires of purest love, what plenitude of bliss is lurking there, for him who dares to gaze unflinching into those mysterious depths ! Where'er that mighty foot shall tread, there structures vainly planned to last for ages shall crumble into ruins . . . and psalms of joy from liberated humanity shall fill the air, still shaken with the din of battle.

Such utterances, it must be owned, sound strange enough in the mouth of one who was actually Master of the Music at a king's Court !

* " Germany and her Princes."

Matters were now moving rapidly to a climax. By
May 3, 1849, it was clear that the extremists had got
the upper hand of the more moderate party. Wagner's
share in the events from May 3 to May 9 has been made
the subject of exhaustive inquiry,[1] and it cannot be
denied that there are grave reasons for suspecting him
of bearing an active part in them.* How far his words
and deeds were actually the result of a deliberately
criminal intention, or merely the hot-headed rashness
of the moment, was of only secondary importance in
the eyes of the judge who tried the case, since similar
excuses might have been urged on behalf of nine-tenths
of the persons involved, especially the great mass of
uneducated and unintelligent hangers-on. With such
people Wagner, as a cultured and highly intellectual
individual, had naturally nothing in common. He
always insisted—and it is evident also from his writings
—that politics for their own sake, the constitutional
side of the republican movement, had comparatively
little interest for him ; revolution was no affair of his,
except for the influence it might be expected to have on
matters artistic. From a radical alteration of social

---

* The war.ant for the arrest of Wagner was in these terms :

WANTED

in connexion with the recent disturbances, in which he is known to have
taken an active part,

RICHARD WAGNER
Court Kapellmeister
of this town.

Age 36 to 37 ; middle height ; brown hair ; wears glasses.

The Police are hereby instructed to look out for the said Wagner, and,
in case of arrest, to report immediately to headquarters.

VON COPPELL
Deputy, City Police
DRESDEN
May 16, 1849

and political conditions he looked for sweeping changes and improvements in the world of art, and this no doubt in his opinion was a high and noble end worth fighting for. But what court of justice, especially at a time of such violent unrest, could be expected to have any sympathy with the crude and muddled ideals of an enthusiast who scarcely knew as yet either what he wanted or how to get it ? The principle that the end justifies the means might well be put forward as a plea in every relation of life, if such frothy notions as these were to be accepted by way either of defence or extenuation.

It is to be noted that Wagner was never actually brought up for examination at the time of the other political trials, for the good reason that he never fell into the hands of the civil power, but contrived to escape by way of Chemnitz to Weimar, and thence to Switzerland. It is true that his name occurs several times in the *dossiers* of other prisoners in con- nexion with various incriminating incidents in his behaviour both before and during the revolution ; but no actual indictment was ever lodged against Wagner himself, with the result that in 1856, when his petition for an amnesty made it necessary to go deeply into the question of his guilt, it was only by examining the *dossiers* of others that a special document dealing with his case could be prepared. Similarly, in the official file that contains his petitions from 1856 to 1860 are to be found a series of classified notes dealing with his offence.[1] From these we learn what charges were officially brought against him and wherein lay the real dangers that he had to fear.

SUMMARY OF EVIDENCE

1. The former Kapellmeister Wagner was intimately acquainted with the leaders of the rising, Bakunin, Heubner, and Röckel.

2. About six weeks before the outbreak of the insurrection secret meetings took place on several occasions at the house of the law-student Neumann,[1] who lived in the Menagerie Garten (so called). Bakunin, who was known as Dr Schwarz, had rooms at that time in Neumann's house. The object of these meetings has not been ascertained, but they are believed to have been connected with the rebellion, as stores of firearms and ammunition are said to have been found on Neumann's premises. Wagner is charged with having been present at these meetings.

3. Wagner is further charged with having lent his garden for the purpose of a conference on the question of arming the populace,[2] in which Röckel, Lieutenants Schreiber and Müller, Professor Semper, and others took part.

4. The notorious brassfounder Oehme, one of those most deeply implicated in the rebellion, and known more particularly for his attempts to burn down the Royal Palace, asserts that just before Easter 1849 Wagner and Röckel gave him an order for a considerable number of hand-grenades ; these were said to be wanted for Prague, and were sent to the office of the *Dresdener Zeitung*. It seems, however, that they were never dispatched to Prague, as Oehme declares that on May 4, 1849, Wagner commissioned him to fill the grenades, which were still at the office of the *Dresdener Zeitung*.[3]

5. Shortly before the outbreak of the rebellion Röckel travelled to Prague, where he endeavoured to arrange for a general armed rising against the various Governments. Meanwhile the Dresden rebellion had broken out, and Wagner wrote to Röckel,* informing him of the fact and

---

* MY DEAR FRIEND,

I hope you have arrived safely in Prague. At the present moment I am thoroughly upset and distracted owing to a long and violent dispute with Könghler and Raty. They have not yet received any definite instructions from

urging him to return.   This letter compromises Wagner in the gravest manner.

6. While the rebellion was in progress Wagner is alleged

(*a*) to have been in the Town Hall on the day of the election of the so-called Provisional Government, and to have incited Bakunin to accompany him ;

(*b*) to have been seen on the Kreuzturm ; and

(*c*) to have accompanied revolutionary reinforcements from Zittau.[1]

7. It is further alleged that, on the return of the insurgents on May 9, 1849, Wagner met Heubner and Bakunin at Tharandt and accompanied them to Freiberg.   It would seem as if Wagner had absented himself from Dresden for a time during the rising, and had been in the country trying to raise reinforcements [2] for the revolutionary cause.[3]

Here, then, we have certain facts which, though they must seem suspicious even to the non-official mind,

Minckwitz ; still, I think you may rest assured that, after the precautionary measures I have taken, there will be no interruption in the progress of events.

Best of friends, do come back as soon as ever your patient can spare you !   Things here look very ugly just now ; all the Unions, the whole of the local militia—who came in this very afternoon—even Prince Albert's regiment, which is stationed here, have declared in the strongest terms or the German Constitution—and the Town Council too is with them.   Everything points to a decisive struggle—if not with the King, at least with the Prussian troops ; the only fear is that a revolution may break out prematurely. Under these circumstances one need not trouble about any reactionary measures on the part of the Government, nor is there any indication that such will be attempted.   Some Hungarian Hussars have arrived in Freiberg from Bohemia, and are kept fully informed of the situation.

In short, the greatest excitement prevails here, and I would earnestly advise you to return *with all speed* to your wife and children, who are naturally much upset.   Otherwise all goes well ;   your wife is in good health, and Schubert is not worrying her ; it is only the political crisis that alarms her and makes her long for her husband's protection.   Moreover, your patients in Limbach must be longing to see you.

Your wife could only get your things to-day, and they are being sent off this evening ; I have refrained from sending the article you particularly requested, for reasons which I think you will approve.   No more at present —only, return as soon as possible !

DRESDEN
May 2, 1849

Yours,
R. W.

23

were never put in evidence, simply because—like Wagner's self-confessed efforts to obtain Tichatschek's rifles for the Vaterlandsverein—they were not discussed at the various trials. Still more incriminating was the printed appeal, or rather summons, directly inspired by Wagner, which was printed in large type on a poster, and placed in a conspicuous position on the barricades, calling on the Saxon troops to make common cause with the insurgents against the Prussian soldiers. Moreover, the fact that he induced Gottfried Semper, the architect, to bring his technical experience to bear on the better construction of the barricades must strike every impartial judge as direct proof of his intention to aid and abet the revolution.

Had Wagner stood his trial the tragic issue in the case of the others makes it fairly certain that he too would have been convicted and possibly condemned to death, as King John points out in a letter to the Grand Duke of Weimar (April 25, 1856).

Even the well-known integrity of the district bailiff, Leonhard Heubner, and his honest endeavours for the common good, could not save him from being sentenced to death, nor could their acknowledged probity avail in the case of Dr Heinrich Herz, the archivist, August Röckel, the conductor, and others who were known to be honest men.

In every instance the death sentence was commuted to penal servitude for life; nevertheless, the terror of death was upon them all. How deeply Wagner was affected by the sentences passed on Röckel, Bakunin, and Heubner is shown by the efforts he made to save them.[1] When Wagner insists, as he always did in later

24

years, that he was blameless of any really criminal act, and had never been detected in any hostile plot against the King, he seems to have but a limited conception of the meaning of guilt. By a guilty person he apparently understands one who fires a pistol at the King or some member of the royal household, sets light to the castle with his own hands, leads the insurgents in person against the royalist troops, or attempts to storm the royal residence. It is true that he had done none of these things, but neither had any of the men already mentioned; what Wagner will not recognize is that the doings referred to in the collected evidence given above are not merely ideal expressions of sympathy with the rebels, but amount to a practical participation in their action. No judge, whether of yesterday or to-day, would be likely to find sufficient grounds for condoning Wagner's lack of common sense and his muddled sense of justice. Even if he had stood his trial ten years later (as he was invited to do) he would probably have been convicted, in spite of the fact that the excitement and bitter feeling in Government circles had given way to a milder, less biased mood than had prevailed in 1849 and 1850.

Although Wagner in his autobiography declares that he had such a vague idea of his position with regard to the legal regulations of his own country that he could not be sure whether he had actually committed a punishable offence, it is possible that his memory, after the lapse of fifteen years, had played him false. We may infer that his intentions were not quite so innocent at the time of the actual events, from his confession that the arrest of Heubner and Bakunin had made such an impression on him that since that time he had allowed no word to escape his lips in connexion with what had happened. Does not this look as if Wagner, if not actually conscious of guilt, was not without a certain guilty feeling ?

For the first few weeks after his flight from Dresden his mood was one of joyful relief over his lucky escape. His stay in Weimar, the thoughtful kindness with which Liszt looked after him, the new friends who rose up on every side with offers of assistance, little excursions like the one to Eisenach, where he was received by the Grand Duchess [1] (the warrant for his arrest had not yet been issued), the visit to the Wartburg, so familiar to him from his own *Tannhäuser*, though he had never seen it—all these things helped to make the present seem bright enough to Wagner, in spite of the gloomier views of his wife, who, sickly, soured, engrossed in the petty cares of everyday, had many a bitter reproach for him on her arrival. When, after a pleasant journey through Thuringia and Bavaria, he took ship at Rorschach and felt the soil of Switzerland under his feet the sense of personal safety gave him a delightful sensation of relief, which was still further increased by his cordial reception in Zürich, where mere acquaintance soon ripened into friendship. His letters to his Dresden friends sound almost exuberantly cheerful. He writes to Theodor Uhlig, a violinist in the royal orchestra at Dresden (April 9, 1849) :

> Freedom, I must frankly confess, is to me the greatest treat of all ! What is the satisfaction of working for the so-called " future of the citizenship " compared with the feeling that one's own noblest activities are no longer hampered by the hand of despotism ! . . . Now that I

KING FREDERICK AUGUST II OF SAXONY

From an oil-painting by Professor Adolf Ehrhardt, painted about 1850,
and presented by him to the city of Dresden.

Municipal Museum, Dresden 26

feel a sense of freedom in my inmost soul, I can snap my fingers at external worries. My life here—where I depend, like a good communist, on Liszt's support—is cheerful, I might almost say happy, and in accordance with the best instincts of my nature.

On September 16 he writes :

I don't know why it is, but I find it impossible to be sad ; especially now my wife is here, and I need not worry about ways and means for the next few months, I feel quite comfortable—nay, overjoyed, like a dog that has got over his thrashing. . . . I desire to be happy, and that one can never be unless one is free—and a man can only be free when he *is* what he *can* and therefore *must* be.

The happy comparison with a whipped hound occurs again in a letter to the Dresden chorus-master, Wilhelm Fischer :

In spite of occasional fits of depression, I feel like a dog that has got over his thrashing ; by " thrashing " I mean the perpetual, senseless, soul-destroying struggle with the impossible, as exemplified in my six years' fight in Dresden against ignorance and insolence. . . . Had I remained there I should have become the helpless victim of spite and calumny.

But now that he has his wife, his dog, and his parrot with him, " the splendid air of Switzerland, the glorious Alpine regions, and a few excellent friends " inspire him with " a sensation of freedom, of untrammelled activity, and a resolute desire to work." So cheerful, indeed, is he that he can joke about his proposed emigration to America. His friend Heine, he says, must not cut him as an American citizen, provided he still wears the old uniform he wore at the Court of Saxony.

This dislike of Dresden, which made him insist so strongly on his present sense of freedom, was mainly due to his chief, the general manager, Wolf von Lüttichau,[1] whom Wagner, after having found in him a patron and benefactor, had come to regard as the cruellest of tyrants; in his autobiography, written many years later, we find the note of bitterness constantly recurring in such expressions as "a person totally devoid of culture," "his cold, reserved manner, his mean insults," "the tyranny of malice and ignorance."[2]

The truth is that, except for a few glorious hours of artistic triumph, Wagner had never been quite happy in his position as Kapellmeister. From first to last he was essentially a creative artist. Interpretation was irksome to him; service of any kind, all regular official duties, repelled him : he regarded them as beneath the dignity of a decent man, more particularly of a creative artist. And yet, in order to maintain himself and his wife, he had to submit to this bondage. Moreover, he had not the usual compensation of the ordinary worn-out office hack whose conscience allows him to reduce his output to the bare necessary minimum ; on the contrary, although he hated it, he had always taken his job as conductor with painful seriousness, and worried himself, as well as his subordinates, into a state of nervous irritation in the endeavour to get everything done in exact accordance with his ideals.[3]

It was not to be expected that Wagner's cheerful mood would be of long duration ; just as a single gleam of light, the faintest glimmer of hope, could set him dreaming of a radiant future and building fantastic castles in the air, so a slight rebuff, a momentary embarrassment, some annoyance or disappointment, was sufficient to bring him down to earth and change the rosy prospect to one of gloom and darkness. So even in Zürich it was not long before the clouds began to gather. Supplies, for which he depended upon his friends, and more particularly Liszt, showed signs of giving out; there was nothing for it but for Wagner to earn money for himself, even at the sacrifice of his scarcely tasted freedom. Urged on by Liszt and Minna, he visited Paris with a view to composing an opera, though he was against the plan from the first, feeling sure, as he did, that what Paris wanted in the way of opera was not his to give. He was soon back again in Zürich; but his health left much to be desired, he was pressed for money, the news from Dresden irritated and enraged him. Mingled with his enthusiasm for freedom and his already rather forced transports at having escaped from the tyrant at Dresden, we soon detect a suspicious strain of pessimism, inclining to a general despair. On June 18, 1849, he had written to Liszt from Rueil, near Paris, begging disconsolately for enough money to keep him for a year —to be provided by benevolent royalties, such as the Grand Duchess of Weimar, the Duke of Coburg, and the Princess Augusta of Prussia. But the very next day he perceives the impossibility of such a plan, considering his present situation. He writes :

Rest assured that the feeling which made me sympathize openly with the Dresden rising was something very different from that absurd fanaticism which sees in every prince merely a creature to be hunted down. You know well that my bitter feelings arose in the first place from matters connected with the practice of my beloved art, and that I nursed them until they spread to all those things which I imagined to be related to the real cause of my profound discontent. The result was that violent mood in which one can only repeat, " There must be a change ! Things cannot go on like this." Now that I have learned the lesson of experience, I need hardly say that never again could I dream of taking part in any political conflict—all my energies are once more absorbed in my art.

There is a touch of bitterness in his letter to Uhlig (November 1849) :

> I am not so cheerful as I was in the summer—autumn and winter are no friends of mine. Moreover, there is always the question of ways and means. . . . I can't think of any way to make money, and all my hopes of assistance have come to nothing.

With bitter irony, too, he writes to Fischer (November 20), " I am face to face with ' the stern realities of life '—that is, I don't quite see how I am to live, for that is what people understand by the phrase nowadays, and nothing else whatever." That was not, however, what Wagner meant by it—material help was always forthcoming.[1] With him it was the struggle for the realization of his artistic ideals, a goal which seemed to him ever beyond his reach, ever more difficult of attainment.

As he had resolved to have nothing more to do with politics, he abstained from full intercourse with his former associates. In Paris, it is true, he met Gottfried Semper, with whom he spent " the only cheerful hours of his stay in that city " ; the rising young scene-painter Heine, to whom he once thought of entrusting the *décor* for *Lohengrin*, being also of the party. But in Zürich he avoided all company of this sort, and so was able to set Minna's fears at rest. " I have nothing to do with the refugees," he writes, " my acquaintances are all Swiss." In a letter to his sister, Clara Wolfram, he is still more emphatic :

> Any reports you may hear of my mixing with the refugees from Saxony,[1] or anywhere else, are false, and the invention of Saxon donkeys. According to my custom, I lead a very retired life, and associate only with certain of the most prominent citizens of Zürich.[2]

In the cheerful and stimulating society of men like Alexander Müller, Wilhelm Baumgärtner, and especially the Public Notaries Jakob Sulzer and Franz Hagenbuch, men of the highest culture, he found everything he wanted. The only 'philistines' of whom he had any knowledge were the refugees from Saxony.

In striking contrast to this aloofness from politics, however, we still find in Wagner a certain tendency to coquette with the outward symbols of revolution. He was always a lover of bright colours, but it is doubtful if this accounts for that marked preference for red which led him to have his collected works bound in that colour, since, in sending his friend Uhlig a manuscript of his *Oper und Drama* bound in red, he deliberately drew attention to his choice of colour. " Red, my friend," he wrote, " represents my principles." The same tendency comes out even more clearly in his letter to Uhlig of December 27, 1849. " So you see I am here in my proper element, since my business is to stir up revolution wherever I go." The work he was planning for Paris was intended to be " merely an incentive to revolution, a plea for the necessity of destruction. Destruction is the one thing needful." This certainly sounds like a genuine echo of Bakunin's ideas, which he had heard so often from the lips of that Russian fanatic. However, it was not really so frightful as all that—it was not to be taken in a political sense; his hostility was directed against the conditions prevailing in the world of the theatre : these were the Augean stables through which he, the modern Hercules, was prepared " ruthlessly to turn the cleansing rivers of pure water." But Wagner, with his impulsive, explosive nature, was utterly devoid of prudence ; such language as this was all very well in confidential letters to his friends, but he would employ it quite recklessly on other occasions, with the result that it soon reached the nervous, suspicious ears of the German, and especially the Saxon, police, thanks to the extensive and well-organized system of espionage maintained by the reactionary Government.

It was just at the beginning of 1851 that the police agencies of Central Europe began to take a lively interest in Wagner's movements.[1] On February 2 of that year Councillor Eberhardt, of Dresden, the editor of the *Allgemeiner Polizei-Anzeiger*, so highly prized in police circles, was approached by the Commissioner of Police at Winnenden with a request for information (dated from Prague on January 31). The document was rather obscurely worded ; a certain Wagner, it seems, who was alleged to have been deeply involved in the Dresden rising and also to have taken an active part in similar disturbances in Austria,[2] had been residing for about a year in Zürich, where he was engaged as conductor to the local theatre. The said Wagner was reported to belong to the leaders of the revolutionary party in Switzerland ; it was further alleged that he was associated with Heimberger,[1] the refugee from Lemberg, and that the two had established relations with Austria. Winnenden requests to be informed whether the individual in question is the same as the well-known Richard Wagner. This communication induced Eberhardt to make inquiries the very next day of the chief of the canton police at Zürich, Captain Nötzli, as to whether Richard Wagner was actually employed as conductor in that town, and if anything else was known about him. Nötzli replied at once in a report, quite characteristic of the official point of view, in which he takes the opportunity to add further details about Wagner, contriving at the same time to associate the composer's name with those of two thoroughly bad characters. The letter is dated February 9, 1851 : [2]

> Richard Wagner, the refugee from Dresden, appears as composer and conductor from time to time, as occasion may demand, at the theatre and the local concerts ; he has no definite appointment. The Jewish swindler, Samuel Lehman, commonly known as Braunschweig, was handed over to the High Court at Hall on February 1. The notorious imposter and forger, Georg Mitalis, *alias* Fürst, from Smyrna, who was expelled from Switzerland for life, will be brought up before the authorities at Basel to-day.

A few weeks later there appeared in No. 73 (March 28, 1851) of the *Neue Preussische Zeitung*, of Berlin, a news-item from Switzerland (dated March 20) to the effect that the Dresden conductor, Wagner, a German refugee, would continue to reside in Zürich,

> where, thanks to his musical abilities, he has succeeded in making his presence very welcome. It would be an exaggeration to regard him as a person of any political importance. As may be seen from his well-known treatise

*Das Kunstwerk der Zukunft,** Wagner is a wild and fantastic idealist, to whom one may fitly apply the well-known saying, " Un homme qui chante n'est jamais dangereux."

The German police, however, were far from taking so benevolent a view of the case ; on the contrary, they continued to keep Wagner under careful supervision.[1]

The end of the year 1851 was marked by a glimmer of hope, difficult to account for and of very short duration. Wagner was taking the cold-water cure at Albisbrunn, a little place at the foot of the Albis range in the canton of Zürich. There, on November 7, while he was actually in his bath, the postmaster from the neighbouring hamlet of Hausen burst excitedly into Wagner's room and showed him the following paragraph in the Zürich *Freitagszeitung* :

> Richard Wagner, who is at present residing in Zürich, has received a full pardon from the King of Saxony. Wagner was sentenced to a long term of imprisonment for having taken part in the May rebellion.[2]

To the postmaster's astonishment Wagner received the news with " the utmost indifference." As he had had no intimation himself, and no official notice had been sent to the Swiss authorities, he decided that it must be a false report. Although it was obvious, from the reference to " a long term of imprisonment," that the paragraph was quite untrustworthy, nevertheless it raised in him some faint hope, to which he hardly liked to confess ; at any rate, he began definitely to consider what he should do " in case there should be something in it." He resolved not to return to Germany, but, after obtaining permission to leave Saxony, to become

* *The Art-work of the Future.*

a Swiss citizen, and so be free to travel where he wished. Although he was forced to regard such an event as very unlikely, he still clung to his hopes, and the discovery that the whole thing was a newspaper *canard* was a bitter blow to him. In a letter to Heine (April 26, 1851) he insists that no one need pity him for having lost his Dresden appointment :

> Were I to be amnestied this very day, you would see with what perfect equanimity I should stay on here in my beloved Switzerland and hardly honour the hallowed soil of Germany with so much as a flying visit.

It is uncertain whether this false rumour was in any way connected with the report that reached Liszt (April 7, 1852) to the effect that Wagner had forwarded a petition for pardon to Dresden. Liszt wrote for a confirmation of this rumour, at the same time expressing his willingness to do his best to help him in the matter. Wagner, however, begged him (April 13) to contradict the report emphatically, else he would be obliged to give a public explanation, which he would rather avoid. He neither intended nor wished to go back to Germany—a visit, *incognito*, to his friends at Weimar was the limit of his desires. But as month after month went by, when supplies began to run short, and there seemed no chance of carrying out his artistic projects, the idea of an amnesty finally gained the upper hand. Of course there was to be no actual surrender.

> My circumstances grow worse from day to day—the life I lead is indescribably futile. If I stay here I shall certainly go under before very long ; and then it will be all too late —too late ! What am I to do ? Must I sue for pardon

from the King of Saxony, or, rather, his ministers—confess my guilt like a humble penitent ?   Can anyone suppose me capable of such a thing ? [1]   Unless Germany opens its doors to me in the near future, if my artistic life is to drag on without sustenance, without stimulus, then the mere animal instinct of self-preservation will drive me to give up art altogether.

II

EARLY ATTEMPTS AT REPATRIATION

1853-55

Wagner's Change of Mood—His Trials as a Composer—Clearing
the Way for the Return to Germany—Minna Wagner's Petition.

AT the beginning of 1853 Wagner's ill-humour
and impatience reached a climax. " This cannot
go on," he writes. " I can bear this life no longer ! "
He urges Liszt to find out definitely whether the Court
of Weimar has any definite plans for procuring his
return to Germany. He has no intention of demean-
ing himself, but will pledge his word to take no further
share in politics. No one but a fool could suppose him
to be a demagogue, to be dealt with as a criminal ; they
were welcome to keep him under police supervision if
they liked, only they must not expect an abject apology
from him. In case of an unfavourable decision he begs
Liszt to be frank with him and let him know without
delay. The only thing then left for him would be to
get hold of sufficient money, by hook or by crook, to
enable him to travel. If even a journey to Spain should
fail to set him up again, " Well, that would be the end
of it—I would rather die than go on living in this
way."

Liszt, with that unfailing tact and thoughtful kindness
which are so pleasing a feature of his association with
Wagner, endeavoured to quiet his excitable friend,
who was always wavering between the extremes

37

of hope and despair, by assuring him of the very favourable disposition of the Court of Weimar. As a matter of fact, the young Charles Alexander (who succeeded to the Grand Dukedom that very summer) was quite willing to use his influence on Wagner's behalf,[1] and seized the opportunity of a visit of the King and Queen of Saxony to Weimar, in June 1853, to plead his cause, but without success. Nevertheless, he did not relax his efforts in Dresden Court circles ; and meanwhile an event happened which seemed to promise a change in the situation.

On December 5, 1852, the King's eldest nephew, Prince Albert, had been betrothed to Princess Carola Wasa, at the castle of Moravetz, in Moravia, and the wedding was to take place in Dresden on July 18, 1853. It had always been the custom in princely houses to make such festivities an occasion for others to share in the rejoicings of the reigning family, particular care being taken to try to brighten, by some special act of grace, the lot of those who were in trouble. No wonder, then, if those who were suffering from the consequences of the May rebellion, as well as their relations and friends, began to cherish new hopes that some ray of light might be thrown upon their darkness. Accordingly, the wife of the conductor, August Röckel (*née* Caroline Lortzing), drew up a petition, in turgid, muddled, almost unintelligible phrases, for the release of her husband, who was in prison at Waldheim, her example being followed by the wives of Hitzschold the bailiff, Gautsch the lawyer, Karl Robert Meier, Burgomaster of Stolpen, the district bailiff, Leonhard Heubner, and others.

Neither Wagner himself nor his wife Minna took any steps at the time, but an attempt seems to have been made in another quarter to get Wagner included in the royal pardon; the composer had still a considerable number of friends and acquaintances in Dresden who would not be likely to neglect so favourable an opportunity of improving his prospects.

But then came the blow. On June 11, 1853, just a week before the day of the wedding, there appeared in Eberhardt's *Allgemeiner Polizei-Anzeiger*, the official organ of the Saxon police, a repetition of the warrant for his arrest issued four years previously.

Wagner, Richard, formerly Kapellmeister in Dresden, one of the most prominent members of the revolutionary party, for whose arrest on account of his share in the Dresden rising in 1849 a warrant was issued, intends, we understand, to leave Zürich, where he is at present residing, and to return to Germany. In order to facilitate his arrest, we publish here a portrait of Wagner. Anyone meeting with this man must arrest him and hand him over to the Royal Court of Justice in Dresden.

The portrait was issued as a supplement with the current number of the *Polizei-Anzeiger*, and is a copy of the original lithograph made by Ernst Kietz in 1842. (In Kietz's sketch Wagner's head is turned to the right, while in the warrant, as reproduced in this volume facing p. 40, it is turned to the left.)

The budding hopes of a general amnesty soon gave way to a feeling of disappointment, which found expression in bitter articles in the Press. In Saxony, where the wave of reactionary feeling was not yet spent, no one ventured to speak out plainly; but we may safely attribute to the influence or instigation of certain well-informed circles in Dresden the article (dated June 17, the day before Prince Albert's wedding) which appeared in the evening edition of the *Zeitung für Norddeutschland* (a Hanover morning paper) on Monday, June 20, and was sent on June 21 by Wermuth, the Chief Commissioner of the Hanover police, to Privy Councillor Ernst Adolph Körner, the head of the second special department, dealing with public order and offences in the Press, attached to the Ministry of the Interior. It runs as follows :

> To-morrow will see the commencement of the festivities for the wedding of Prince Albert of Saxony and Princess Carola Wasa, the lady with whom an alliance was once so strongly desired by the Emperor-elect of the French.[1] Those good souls who anticipated some gracious concession in favour of the still large number of political prisoners will find themselves doubly disappointed. Of those condemned for the May rising alone a hundred and nine are still detained in Saxon prisons ; moreover, the trials following on subsequent denunciations in connexion with that event seem never ending, and have only lately resulted in a number of sentences of imprisonment, both in Wurzen and Leipzig. The so-called *Freimüthige Sachsenzeitung*, which is actually the organ of the Court party, excels all others in this campaign of hatred and malice. How far this party is prepared to go is shown by a signed article that appeared only the other day in a public journal, by the county court assessor, Pechmann, a magistrate who happened to have fallen under their displeasure. In their opinion, he says, "political prisoners were to be treated as something less than human beings." The country will the more fully appreciate the nature of the disappointment in store for them when it reads to-morrow how Prince Albert (whose interests are purely military) has granted an amnesty to a number of the soldiers condemned for participating in the events of last May, besides showing extraordinary leniency to the remainder.

Extra-Beilage zu Eberhardt's Allgem. Polizei-Anzeiger.
Band XXXVI. N.º 47.

Richard Wagner

*ehmal Capellmeister und politischer
Flüchtling aus Dresden*

THE PORTRAIT OF WAGNER ON THE WARRANT

From the lithograph on the reissued warrant of 1853 in Eberhardt's *Algemeiner Polizei-Anzeiger*, edited by Police-Assessor Hermann Müller.

State Archives Library, Dresden

This article was followed immediately by a copy of the warrant for arrest in the *Polizei-Anzeiger* quoted above. Wermuth had suggested in his letter that the publication of this document pointed to a want of discretion in certain quarters, seeing that Eberhardt's *Polizei-Anzeiger* was accessible only to a limited circle of readers, and was not meant for the general public. On the following day, however, immediately after the receipt of this letter and the newspaper, Körner furnished his colleague in Hanover with the necessary explanation :

> The communication to the *Freimüthige Sachsenzeitung* of the extract from the *Polizei-Anzeiger* concerning Richard Wagner was not a violation of any official secret : it was done expressly at my request. We have here a fairly strong and active party so interested in Wagner as to be working not only for his pardon, but also for his restoration some day to his former position. There is no immediate fear of the latter ; but seeing that pardon has been granted to so many other traitors, we cannot altogether ignore the possibility of Wagner being included in the number of the pardoned, especially on the eve of his Royal Highness's wedding, when many are looking forward to the granting of pardons on an extensive scale. Partly in order to stop the spread of such hopes and so prevent an unfortunate disappointment, partly also to upset the activities of the pro-Wagner party, it seemed desirable to draw public attention once more to the existence of the warrant for arrest; in any case, the interests of the State will be sufficiently served if we succeed in making Wagner afraid to set foot again in Germany.
>
> Furthermore, it is clear that the correspondent of the *Zeitung für Norddeutschland* has copied from the *Freimüthige Sachsenzeitung*, since the issue of that paper dated June 17 actually appeared about six o'clock in the evening of June 16. That the *Sachsenzeitung* was the first to give

publicity to the warrant was purely accidental, and due to the fact that, though the report was obviously no secret, still the official Dresden journal did not seem the proper vehicle for its publication. In any case, though the incident fails to put us on the track of the local correspondent, I am very grateful to you for the courtesy you have shown in the matter.

DRESDEN
June 22, 1853

What justification there may have been for the apprehension aroused in Court and Government circles respecting a possible amnesty for Wagner cannot now be ascertained; but it is certain that the resumption of the performances of *Tannhäuser* on October 26, 1852, strengthened both the hopes and fears of the respective parties. Wagner's friends saw in it the possibility of a pardon or even of a reconciliation with the Royal Family, while his enemies feared a renewal of those disturbing elements which they thought had been laid to rest. It was well understood that the King was sufficiently impartial to discriminate between the man and his work, and was fond of hearing Wagner's music performed; still, the fact that an opera by an outlawed man had been restored to the *répertoire* of the Royal Court Theatre, where it had five performances, coupled with the resentment shown toward a reactionary paper which opposed these performances, did seem to point to something more than a mere personal partiality for the new development in music, something, in fact, that called for prompt and vigorous action. The whole conduct of the police in this matter, as described in their records with an astonishing, almost cynical effrontery, has rather the air of being a carefully prepared campaign. One might almost fancy that the alleged anxiety was to a great extent only a pretext, and that the reissuing of the warrant was not really an answer or a counterstroke to the movement in favour of an amnesty, but that some power in the Government, or, at least, in high official circles, mindful of the time-honoured axiom, " A thrust is the best parry," aimed at extinguishing the last spark of hope before it could break into even a tiny flame. At the same time a check was put upon the more lenient impulses of the King, who could not go counter to those whom he knew to be the most faithful supporters of his throne. The hypothesis of a deliberately planned attack is strengthened by the fact that the Dresden police, not content with a single blow, took pains to secure the widest possible publicity for the issue of the warrant, and rejoiced in their success. In the "confidential communications" issued by headquarters at Dresden to other police authorities and their agents outside Saxony we find (No. XI, Dresden, August 5, 1853) a concise statement of the facts of the case, as well as of the precautions taken to thwart Wagner's alleged intention of giving concerts in Germany, and a fresh expression of satisfaction that the *coup* had succeeded :

On the occasion of the marriage of his Royal Highness Prince Albert exaggerated rumours were set on foot of a general amnesty for the rebels and traitors who are still in prison ; this was done either with the purpose of aiding the efforts of those who were working for the release of the most dangerous leaders of that party, or, failing this, in the hope of stirring up discord. Seeing that Richard Wagner, who is the favourite subject for exploitation by the democratic party, was just at that time desirous of repeating on German soil the concerts he had given in Zürich, it was, in a sense, as an answer to the rumours of pardon that the copy of the warrant against Wagner—issued in 1849, but never put into execution—appeared in Eberhardt's *Allgemeiner Polizei-Anzeiger*. This expedient, thanks to the active co-operation of the entire German Press, achieved its twofold purpose ; not only were the rumours and hopes of pardon effectually quashed, but Richard Wagner himself abandoned his project for a concert tour in Germany, and now intends, it is said, to visit St Moritz in the Engadine, in the company of his niece and his friend Franz Liszt, from Weimar.

This last statement, about the journey to St Moritz, was taken from an official communication addressed by the Vienna police to Körner (July 1, 1853) :

According to information received, Richard Wagner, the political refugee, has no immediate intention of going to Germany ; indeed, he is expecting his friend Liszt from Weimar, in whose company (and that of his own niece, who has just arrived in Zürich from London) he will leave for St Moritz in the Engadine.[1]   He was highly flattered on hearing that the warrant for his arrest had been printed in the *Polizei-Anzeiger*, and is said to take no little pride in the fact that he is described as a prominent supporter of the revolutionary party.[2]   It is a mystery where Wagner gets the money for his extravagant way of living, as he does not earn a penny in Zürich.   They say he has had 150 copies of his latest works printed at his own expense, some of them magnificently bound for presentation.[3] . . . With regard to Wagner, we shall send the necessary notice to the Tyrol police to have him kept under observation during his stay in the neighbourhood of the Imperial frontiers.

Vienna
July 1, 1853

When Liszt was in Zürich Wagner had assured him that he had finally said good-bye to politics of any sort, and begged him to impress the fact upon other people, especially those in influential positions.   However, we find Liszt writing from Frankfurt (July 12, 1853) to the effect that neither of the two persons to whom he had spoken on the matter would believe his statements as to Wagner's non-political attitude. Remembering where the letter was written, we may assume that Liszt is referring not to the members of the royal house at Weimar, but probably to the Regent, Frederick of Baden, in Karlsruhe.

According to agreement, Wagner had sent a letter intended for the young Grand Duke, Charles Alexander, to his friend at Vienna, who, while on a visit to Ettersburg Castle, near Weimar, found an early opportunity to deliver it.[1] That Wagner's political trustworthiness was gravely suspected—and that not in Germany only—is evident from the difficulty he had in procuring a French visa for a journey to Paris ; he was obliged to present himself at the French Embassy in Berne in order to remove the suspicions to which false reports had given rise. The Ambassador even offered to report favourably to the Government in Paris, but the affair dragged on until Wagner was compelled to ask Liszt to plead his cause with the French Embassy at Karlsruhe.[2] This continued mistrust on the part of the various Governments at that time is explained by the bad reputation which still clung to him, owing to his implication in the May revolution, which was further strengthened by the reissue of the warrant for his arrest. Moreover, the confidential communications exchanged between the police authorities of the different states helped to perpetuate the ill-feeling against him. Fresh ground for suspicion was also found in the character of the people with whom

Wagner was associating, for this, like everything else relating to the refugees, was reported to the Dresden police by the agents employed by them in every country.

Particularly suspicious, for instance, must have appeared his association with Georg Herwegh, a most obnoxious person, notorious as the author of *Gedichte eines Lebendigen*, with whom Wagner was for a long period on the most familiar footing. In Paris, in 1850, his companions were Gottfried Semper and the young Wilhelm Heine, son of his friend Friedrich Heine and one of the Dresden refugees ; while in Zürich he was known to be in touch with the lawyer Marschall von Bieberstein, formerly an officer in the Dresden town guard, who had taken part in the May revolution.[1] Further, in 1852, he had been in correspondence with the notorious Malvida von Meysenbug, who had made herself known to him as a revolutionary extremist, and who was constantly under police supervision as the friend and *confidante* of the dreaded Italian conspirator Giuseppe Mazzini.[2] Finally, his acquaintance with Eduard Rémenyi, the Hungarian violinist, was yet another ground for suspicion, since the latter had attracted the especial attention of the police as a well-known adherent of the revolutionary party.[3]

A man who, after being heavily involved in the Dresden revolution, still persisted in associating with so many suspicious, or even disreputable, characters could hardly be regarded by the authorities as a harmless person. We must bear in mind the political mentality, the intellectual stagnation, of most of the Governments of Germany at that time, still suffering as they were from the shock of the upheaval of 1848–49, in order to understand what seems to us the almost ludicrous terror attaching to the word 'demagogue' in the fifties; it would certainly have been impossible to convince these one-ideaed officials that Wagner's intercourse with these suspicious persons was merely that of man with man or of one musician with another. The consequence was that Wagner, equally with the other refugees, revolutionaries, and democrats, was kept for many years under the surveillance of detectives, who, linked together by a common aim, zealously imparted to each other the information they collected about him. Even as a conductor his activities were regarded as dangerous; who could be sure that the villain, under the pretence of raising his baton, might not proceed to fling hand-grenades among the audience? Had he not in his time placed an order for those deadly weapons with the Dresden brassfounder Oehme?

At the beginning of 1854 information was received at Dresden that Wagner intended to visit Munich. Against this danger to the peace of the community Privy Councillor Körner considered it necessary to take precautions, and on January 16, 1854, he wrote directly to the chief of the Munich police, Councillor von Döring:

> As reported in the newspapers, Richard Wagner, late Kapellmeister in Dresden, for whose arrest a warrant was issued on May 15, 1849, has been invited by the superintendent of the Court Theatre, Dr Dingelstedt,[1] to go to Munich, in order to produce his opera *Tannhäuser*. Should this be true, I rely upon your Honour, in accordance with the terms of the warrant above mentioned, to

arrest Wagner on the spot, and to report the same to headquarters here. . . .

<small>DRESDEN</small>
16, i, 54

The Dresden police were not left long in uncertainty. On January 22 a reassuring reply arrived from von Döring to the effect that

> the report that the well-known composer Richard Wagner has been invited by the superintendent of the Court Theatre to conduct his opera *Tannhäuser* in this city is without foundation.[1] Wagner is not in Munich, but should he arrive here, contrary to expectation, I will not fail to put the Dresden warrant into execution.

The Dresden police, as it happened, had to content themselves with this assurance, since the opportunity for action never occurred.

There is no doubt that about this time Wagner had a great desire to get back to Germany, if only on a flying visit ; he regarded an amnesty as indispensable, and his mind was full of all sorts of plans for the future, as we see clearly from his intimate correspondence with Liszt. In February 1854, when the negotiations with Breitkopf and Härtel over the publication of *Lohengrin* had broken down, and the performance of that opera in Leipzig had not met with the decided success for which he had hoped, he wrote to Liszt :

> And that is why I have been possessed of late with a stronger desire than ever to procure an amnesty, and so have free access once again to Germany. There at least I could be usefully employed in superintending the performances of my operas ; I could at last produce *Lohengrin* myself, whereas at present it is torture to me even to think of it. For the moment it seemed to me that the most essential thing of all was to wipe out the disaster

at Leipzig. I very nearly risked my freedom (freedom, indeed! what irony!) by venturing on the journey without a passport. In calmer moments I resolved to write to the King of Saxony—until that idea in turn came to seem futile, or even unworthy. Lastly—that is, up to last night—I thought of writing to the Grand Duke, explaining my new position, in the hope of inducing him to wake matters up in Dresden, but this morning, I must confess, that too seems useless—and I daresay you are of the same opinion.

He must have changed his mind, however, as to the proposed letter to the King of Saxony, for in April we find him writing to Liszt:

Would it be any good if I were to send you a letter for the King of Saxony which the Grand Duke of Weimar might present to him through a confidential agent—perhaps his Ambassador? I grant that the Secretary of State might be more useful to me even than the King, but I cannot possibly approach a man like that. Do you think the Duke would consent?

Liszt, the model of calm deliberation, found himself once more in the painful position of having to tell the plain truth to his too sanguine friend, in spite of his inclination to conceal it. He replied:

After my own experiences (of which I have told you only a small part) I very much doubt if the King will grant the favour we desire. Still, I will make one more attempt. Send me your letter for his Majesty, and I shall hope to get it presented through the best possible channel. Our Grand Duke is away just now, so I shall not be able to speak to him before some time next week. Write me at once, and direct your letter to Dresden.

But in the meantime Wagner had changed his mind. On May 2 he writes as follows:

I think it best to give up all idea of writing to the King. I really don't see how I could put the truth before him

in a way he would understand ; and I will not tell a lie—
that is about the only sin I recognize !

In the spring of 1854 the following interesting report
was circulated by the Vienna police in their " confidential communications " for March 23, and reached
Dresden on the 28th. It shows how well the police
were kept informed of every circumstance of Wagner's
daily life and actions, although the truth was often
distorted in the transit, and anything that was particularly to his disadvantage was eagerly seized upon
and served up without proof or examination.

We hear strange reports about Richard Wagner at
Zürich. He not only lives in ostentatious luxury, but is
purchasing the most valuable articles, such as gold watches,
at extravagant prices. His apartments are furnished in
magnificent style, with carpets, silk curtains, and chande-
liers, all of the finest. The simple sons of the republic
look on astonished, and cannot help wondering where
the man gets his money from, as he was quite poor when
he came to Zürich. He gives out that he makes a lot of
money from the performance of his operas in Germany,
but, on strict investigation, this has been found to be un-
true. The few theatres which venture to perform them
pay him nothing,[1] nor can his writings bring him in anything, since he prints only fifty to a hundred copies of a
work, and those at his own expense. In Zürich not only
does he make nothing by his operas, he even spends
money in order to stimulate public interest. There are
strong reasons, therefore, for supposing that he is secretly
subsidized by one of the princely houses of Germany ; this
is all the more amazing since it is known that not only did
he set fire to the wardrobe of the theatre at the time of the
Dresden revolution,[2] but is still trying by his speeches and
his writings to bring about a revolutionary movement by
means of his art,[3] and to this end is in communication
with all the literary and artistic forces of revolutionary
propaganda.

FRANZ LISZT

FRANZ LISZT

From an engraving bearing the words, " Drawn by W. Kaulbach, engraved by C. Gonzenbach." Under it is an inscription in Liszt's handwriting to Gottfried Semper, Wagner's fellow-revolutionary and fellow-exile: " Let us be Poly-chromists and keep our colour and line. F. Liszt, to his honoured friend Semper." Karl Gonzenbach, the engraver, lived at Munich after 1838.

Belief in his " music of the future " is notably on the wane, as it becomes more and more evident that his works, in spite of their brilliant orchestration, possess neither soul nor melody—what melodies are to be found in them he has stolen from others.

Meanwhile Wagner was perpetually dissatisfied with the existing position. Now that he had ceased for a time his activities as an author and was once more engaged on actual composition his remoteness from any of the leading centres of art was a source of even greater regret. Toward the end of 1853, after an interval of more than five years, he again set to work on *Das Rheingold*, to be followed in the summer and autumn of 1854 by *Die Walküre*. In order to ensure greater peace at home and fewer distractions, he arranged that his wife should go for a time to her family in Saxony. Her tour, beginning at Zwickau and including a visit to Liszt in Weimar, turned Wagner's thoughts once more in the direction of an amnesty. He wrote to Minna [1] that her letter had increased his longing to make music in his own way.

As time goes on my detention in Zürich becomes a torture which would be intolerable were it not for my proud determination not to yield. I confess that if the Grand Duke of Weimar were this day to obtain permission for me to reside in his territory unmolested, I should probably not hesitate long before accepting his offer. If you agree with me as to the desirability of our settling down in some place where I should be more or less within reach of the artistic materials necessary for my work, I give you full liberty to confer with Liszt as to the possibility of obtaining such permission. In my opinion the only way would be for the Grand Duke to appeal directly to the King of Saxony to allow me to live unmolested in his (the Duke's) country, I, on my side, undertaking not to leave it without the Duke's permission. At the same time I am prepared to give a formal promise to take no further part in politics ; only, with reference to the past, I must be excused those judicial proceedings which, besides being humiliating, might easily place my conduct in a false light.

I cannot exist much longer in a place like this, where there is nothing whatever to stimulate my artistic powers. You know how in these last years I have always cherished a hope that it would be possible for me to do something here for music, and I may truly say that I have done my best to this end—but the results show that these people are impossible. . . . So long as I was writing books, and then my poems, this place was tolerable, but for the past year, since I have begun to compose again, the absolute artistic stagnation of my surroundings has had a most depressing effect upon me. This is already noticeable in my work ; my pleasure in it is steadily declining, and I fear, if this goes on much longer, I shall again give up composition. It is really too vexatious.

Wagner's suggestion fell flat. We can hardly suppose that Minna—when we consider her subsequent move in Dresden—did not move in the matter ; it is more likely that Liszt still had scruples about worrying the Duke afresh with the same troublesome business. In Weimar, moreover, they were better informed than in Zürich as to the state of feeling in the higher circles of Dresden. The reigning monarch, John, who, on August 9, 1854, had succeeded his brother, Frederick Augustus II, was known to be a great stickler for maintaining the letter of the law, and less inclined to leniency than his milder-natured predecessor, with his well-known liking for Wagner's music.[1]

In spite of her original intention to avoid Dresden, and invite her parents to join her at Zwickau, Minna

journeyed to the capital in October without informing
her husband.   On her arrival she ventured on a course
of action likely, as she thought, to forward Wagner's
interest, and, in accordance with the suggestions contained in his letter to her, she presented a petition pray-
ing that her husband might be allowed to be present at
performances of his own works in Germany.   With
her rather muddled way of reasoning, she may well
have believed that her plea for pity would be sure to
touch the heart of the King ; it never occurred to her
that an entirely unsupported appeal, as this was, could
have no chance of success with a ruler like King John,
who, though by no means unfeeling in his private
relations, was known for his cool judgment in his
capacity of statesman and chief guardian of the law.

The petition was sent about the middle of October :

May it please your Majesty !

Emboldened by your Majesty's well-known bene-
volence and nobility of character, I have come a long
journey humbly to crave your Majesty's pardon and forgiveness for a banished man whose works at one time had
the good fortune to enjoy your Majesty's favour.   The
wife of Richard Wagner, now in exile, throws herself at
your Majesty's feet and implores you, as the protector of
the arts and sciences, to show mercy to an erring artist
who is in despair at finding his activities hampered by the
fact that he is never able to hear his own compositions.
May your Majesty be graciously pleased to pardon my
husband, the misguided Richard Wagner, and allow him
to be present when his own works are performed, that he
may feel encouraged by your Majesty's gracious magna-
nimity to proceed with his work as a composer !

I have only most humbly to beg your Majesty's indulgence for a sorely tried woman who ventures to appeal to
your Majesty's generosity on behalf of one who has erred,

and who finds this hindrance to the exercise of his art so heavy a penalty.

Your Majesty's most humble and
deeply afflicted servant,
MINNA WAGNER

On October 26 the King gave orders that the document should be forwarded to the Ministry of Justice, where it was received the following day. On November 27 the Minister of Justice, Zschinsky,[1] having first ascertained the King's opinion, as was customary in such cases, gave his decision, with the direction that it was to be handed to the petitioner on her personal application. But Minna had not to wait so long ; after some little time had elapsed and the document still remained uncalled for it was forwarded to her on December 13. The reply was short and to the point :

> The petition for pardon addressed to the King by Minna Wagner on behalf of her husband, Richard Wagner, a fugitive from justice under suspicion of high treason, has been handed to the Ministry of Justice in accordance with his Majesty's instructions. As, however, it would be a grave responsibility to advise his Majesty to show any clemency in the case of one who is still a fugitive and has never stood his trial, the petitioner is informed that her appeal is rejected.

Minna had already returned to Zürich when this decision reached her. After so long a silence she can scarcely have expected any reply, so that the shock of the refusal was probably not so great. Whether she kept it to herself, whether the Master ever came to know of his wife's fruitless effort, we cannot tell ; neither in his autobiography nor in those letters to his friends that have been published is there any mention

MINNA WAGNER
From the engraving made by Weger at Leipzig, which was based upon
a photograph.
Municipal Museum, Dresden   54

of this first attempt to win over the authorities in Saxony.

Remembering Wagner's constant changes of mood and the consequent violent contradictions that occur in his utterances, we need not be surprised to find him writing to Fischer on August 8, 1854, that he " had no desire to go to Germany ; he was glad, indeed, that he could not be present at the miserable performances of his operas given there, which would probably break his heart "—and this only a short time after his appeal to his wife to endeavour, with Liszt's help, to obtain permission for his return !

In January 1855 he undertook to conduct a series of concerts in London. This was a kind of work he had always detested, but he hoped he might find some compensation for the hopeless outlook in Germany by enlisting the sympathy of England for his artistic schemes. It is in this mood that he writes to Fischer from Paris, on his way to London (March 2, 1855) :

> I shall probably never go back to Germany. You are all so silent about my prospects there that I can only conclude there is no hope for me. Well, if such is the will of our noble Government I must get used to it.

But though he may try to persuade his friends, and even himself, that he has finished with Germany, we feel how heavily the hopelessness of his present position weighs upon him ; he may talk contemptuously of " getting used to it," but the whole passage shows how very far he was from being truly resigned. It is certain that his stay of nearly four months in London served to dispel any illusions he may have had as to the English. In a letter to Fischer on March 26 he groans aloud, " To-day is my second concert. . . . The choirs here are wretched ! If I could only have my Palm Sunday singers from Dresden ! "

The only ray of light in this unhappy London episode was the visit of Queen Victoria and the Prince Consort to the seventh concert on June 11, an event which was very gratifying to him for political reasons, especially as Prince Albert himself was of the house of Wettin.[1] In his letters to Minna and Fischer he goes into the details of the affair with evident satisfaction, and does not fail to draw attention to the grotesque paradox that he, " the arch-traitor against whom a warrant was still out, should be conducting a concert in the presence of Victoria and her Court." It is significant that his thoughts turn at once to the treatment he had received from his own country, which, he writes, " might well follow such an example." This, however, Germany was not prepared to do, though his London trip had excited a good deal of not altogether favourable attention. The French Ambassador had begun by raising difficulties about the passport, and had consulted the Government in Paris, which shows that Wagner was still an object of suspicion in that capital. However, Liszt intervened on his friend's behalf, and the journey took place without further hindrance. But rumours of the initial difficulties had found their way into Germany, as will be seen from the following article which appeared in No. 62 of *Didaskalia*, the supplement to the *Frankfurter Journal* of March 13, 1855 :

It is probable that Richard Wagner will have to extend his journey from Zürich to London by a lengthy *détour*.

The French Ambassador in Berne has refused to visé his passport, so that if Wagner is still determined to fulfil his concert engagements in the English capital he will have no alternative but to sail from Genoa.

This silly paragraph was contradicted as soon as it appeared by the established fact that Wagner had been in London since March 4. Even here his movements were carefully watched. When, after the fourth concert, Wagner, furious at the arrangement of the programme, announced his intention of returning to the Continent, a singer who happened to be present (a young German Jew, says Wagner in a letter to Fischer) took the trouble to spread the news. His opponents seized upon the report, and No. 119 of the *Dresdener Journal* came out with the following statement :

LONDON

Richard Wagner, dissatisfied with his reception in England, has given up the conductorship of the Philharmonic Concerts, and left the country.

In this case also the malicious rumour was contradicted—by the immediate adjustment of the quarrel— before it had time to appear in the German papers, yet it was eagerly repeated throughout the country, and an echo of it is found in the weekly notes of the Dresden police during May 1855 : "It is said that Kinkel is returning to Zürich, together with Richard Wagner, whose departure from London has already been reported." In another note the return is spoken of as an accomplished fact : "Kinkel is said to be residing at present in Switzerland, having accompanied Richard Wagner on his return from London."

In spite of these reports, which, as we have seen,

were promptly seized upon by Wagner's enemies, the composer remained a full month longer in London, returning to Zürich on June 30.[1]   However much the disillusionment of his London experiences might incline Wagner to pine for his " beloved and glorious Switzerland," which he hopes " never again to leave," and to declare that nothing should ever again lure him from his retirement amid the beauties of nature or from his work, " which is the only real substance of life," he did not remain long in this mood.   On August 17, 1855, we find him writing to his friend Fischer, in a strain that is meant to be playful, " I have no news for you—except that the King intends to grant me an amnesty very shortly."   But at the end of the letter the old bitterness breaks out again :

> What do the good folk in Dresden say when they hear of my *Tannhäuser* being given again in Munich ?   Do they take a malicious pleasure in still preventing me from being present at the performances ?   I expect they do !

III

ROYAL INTERVENTION
1855–57

The Grand Duke Charles Alexander of Weimar intercedes—
Wagner's Appeal to King John.

WAGNER'S time was now fully occupied. He was engaged with the score of *Die Walküre*, as well as the libretto of *Tristan* and another poem called *Die Sieger*, based on an Indian legend. Moreover, his social circle was enlarged by the addition of Gottfried Semper, who was now settled at Zürich as a teacher in the Polytechnic, and of Gottfried Keller, and he was sadly interrupted by repeated attacks of erysipelas. The year 1856 opened with money troubles, and Liszt, always ready to help to the best of his ability, came to his assistance, although his own financial position gave him much anxiety at the time.

Meanwhile, at the approach of spring, the thought of a return to Germany again revived, and with such violence that he determined on the very step from which he had hitherto recoiled—a personal appeal to the King of Saxony. He was further encouraged by a suggestion from the Chief of Police at Prague— always well disposed to him—that he should become a naturalized Swiss, and then apply for a passport to Austria, where he would then be able to reside without any fear of Saxony, since " Richard Wagner, a Saxon subject," would no longer exist. The plan struck

Wagner as a good one, but it seemed to him of still greater importance to procure the right of entry into Germany, not with a view to permanent residence— for that he preferred some quiet spot in Switzerland— but in order that he might attend the performances of his operas, especially *Lohengrin*, in Berlin and Munich. For the rehearsals of *Die Nibelungen*, too, a residence in Germany was absolutely indispensable, and finally his desire to be near Liszt had great weight with him. On April 13 he writes to the latter :

> I cannot go on any longer without taking some decided step toward this goal, so I have determined to approach the King of Saxony with a view to an amnesty, frankly setting forth the reasons for my urgent need, and at the same time giving my word of honour that never again will I take part in any political movement.

Wagner seems honestly to have believed that this first humble gesture on his part was all that was necessary ; it scarcely occurred to him that the Saxon Government might be altogether disinclined to grant his request. His only fear—quite an unjustifiable one—was lest "the other side" (*i.e.,* the King and Government) might publish his letter with the object of humiliating him. However unfriendly the attitude of the Government may have been, to suppose King John capable of so mean an act was unworthy not only of the monarch, but of the artist as well. The reissue of the warrant of 1853 had left a painful impression, but, as we have seen, this was exclusively the work of the police in conjunction with a hostile clique. That there was no general ill-feeling toward Wagner in Dresden is proved (to say nothing of the performance of *Tannhäuser* in 1852, mentioned above) by the records of the theatrical authorities ; on the many occasions during the years from 1851 to 1856 when they were approached by other theatres with requests for the loan of scores and orchestral parts of Wagner's operas and concert pieces, not only did they willingly consent so far as they were able, but they also showed a proper regard for the composer's rights by pointing out that it was necessary first to obtain his permission.

His groundless fears of betrayal by the Saxon authorities led Wagner to propose that Liszt, backed by a letter from the Grand Duke, should obtain an audience of King John, in the course of which he was to set forth Wagner's artistic standpoint, and at the same time explain and excuse his political attitude, making it clear that he was prepared for the future to keep himself in the background, and refrain from any sort of political controversy.   Wagner wrote :

> All this you could explain much more simply and clearly by word of mouth than I could by letter, especially in the form of a petition.   I earnestly entreat you to do me this great kindness—spare two days at Dresden for my sake, and set to work with all the energy the affair demands. . . . You are the only one who can properly plead my cause ; should you have any reason for refusing, my only alternative would be to write to the King myself.   In that case the question arises, whom should I get to present my letter ?   The Weimar Ambassador, perhaps ?   Should the King reject my petition, there still remains the offer made to me by a certain Prussian Minister to intervene on my behalf.

However much he might sympathize with Wagner, Liszt had excellent reasons for refusing this request ; his knowledge of the world, his experience of Courts, had taught him the impossibility of such methods, more

particularly in the case of a sovereign like John, whose
whole nature would revolt at any such attempt to force
his hand. Accordingly he wrote at once to his im-
petuous friend, urging him to reject the idea of an
intermediary.

> My sole advice to you is that you send in your petition
> to the King of Saxony without delay ; in the present state
> of your affairs such a step is absolutely necessary, and you
> may be sure I should not press you to take it were I not
> quite convinced that there is no other way of procuring
> your return to Germany.[1]

However, in spite of this advice, Liszt did not remit
his own efforts. He persuaded the Grand Duke to
make strong representations to the King—not, indeed,
on the lines Wagner had proposed—in the following
letter (April 20) :

> Your Majesty will hardly be surprised if the recollection
> of your kindness on former occasions emboldens me to
> ask yet another favour. I can only hope your Majesty
> will pardon me on learning that I plead on behalf of a
> guilty man—doubly guilty where your Majesty is con-
> cerned. Yet, in consideration of his undoubtedly sincere
> repentance and of the extraordinary artistic gifts which it
> has pleased an all-merciful God to bestow upon him, I do
> not hesitate to bring to your Majesty's notice the name of
> Richard Wagner ; and I do so with the more confidence
> as it is not so much for his pardon that I plead as for per-
> mission to reside for a certain period unmolested in Ger-
> many, in order to be present at the performance of his
> own works. Of the reputation these have won for him
> I need not speak, nor of how desirable it is that he should
> be able to continue his career ; but your Majesty, as an
> enlightened patron of the arts, will agree that for the artist,
> and especially for the composer, no progress is possible
> unless he is able to take the measure of himself, to learn his
> own powers, or—in the present case—to hear his own
> works. In the place where he is now living there is no

THE GRAND DUKE CHARLES ALEXANDER OF
WEIMAR

From *Gedenkschrift zur Erinnerung an den Grossherzog Carl Alexander*
(Weimar, 1918). Reproduced from the portrait (1856) by Richard
Lauchert at Weimar. The original is in the possession of the Grand
Ducal family.

opportunity for Wagner to enjoy these advantages—Germany is the only country where that is possible ; hence his most earnest desire to obtain your Majesty's forgiveness and permission to return for a season to his native land. This desire he has from time to time, and indirectly, made known to me. For reasons which your Majesty will understand I have hesitated hitherto to take notice of his appeals ; I am moved to do so now—apart from the immediate motive—because, like your Majesty, I consider the exercise of mercy to be our noblest privilege. Therefore I beseech your Majesty graciously to allow Wagner to reside for a time in this town for the purpose above mentioned, and, further, to instruct your Majesty's Embassy at Court to inform my Government of this act of grace.

Please present my homage to her Majesty the Queen, and believe me to be

Your devoted cousin and servant,
CHARLES ALEXANDER

WEIMAR
April 20, 1856

To this request the King replied without consulting any of his advisers ; both the rough draft and the fair copy of his letter are in his own handwriting :

MOST GRACIOUS LORD AND DEAREST COUSIN,

I hasten to reply to your valued letter of the 20th with the frankness which is customary between kinsmen.

I will begin by remarking that I should never dream of trying to influence your Royal Highness's decision in the matter in hand, since obviously the question of whom you may choose to allow to reside within the state of Weimar is entirely your own affair. When, however, your Royal Highness expresses a desire for direct intervention on my part I venture to think that you may not be fully informed as to Wagner's position and previous record, or you would see reasons for modifying your opinion.

Wagner came to Dresden as a penniless composer of

63

whom nobody had heard, and obtained permission to produce his *Rienzi*. My late brother, quick to recognize the remarkable talent which the work revealed, was induced to make Wagner his Kapellmeister, to satisfy his creditors, and thus raise him from a state of grinding poverty to a position at once honourable and—had he so willed it—free from all anxiety.

In return for all these benefits [1] Wagner, in the years 1848–49, incited the members of his orchestra to rebel against the Court, and finally took an active part in the memorable May rebellion; had he not fled the country, he would probably have been condemned to death for high treason.

It is obvious that no talent, however great, can compensate for such ungrateful and scandalous behaviour; moreover, I should not feel justified in extending any special favour to Wagner, to the exclusion of his fellow-culprits who are still undergoing the heavy punishments incurred.

Whether, under these circumstances, it would be consistent with the dignity of your Court, and with its relation with a friendly state, to receive such a man as Wagner, I may fairly leave to your Majesty's own good feeling. I hope, my dear cousin, that you will forgive my plain speaking, especially when I tell you that I have written this letter without consulting anyone; on so delicate a point I judged it best to speak my mind freely as a friend and cousin, rather than to invite the opinion of a third person.

Assuring you of my continued goodwill as friend and kinsman, I am, dearest cousin,

Your Royal Highness's most devoted

JOHN

DRESDEN
April 25, 1856

Nothing could be clearer than the drift of this reply. The polite suggestion at the beginning that the Grand Duke is free to act as he will is practically cancelled by the unconditional refusal to accede to his request;

indeed, by his allusion to the relations between the two Courts the King not only puts any favourable solution out of the question, but even manages to convey a hint of reproach. It would seem that the Duke, who in spite of this rebuff was by no means prepared to abandon Wagner's cause, said nothing at the time to Liszt, who would have been sure to inform his friend. Meanwhile Wagner, ignorant of what had passed, resolved, though with a heavy heart, to write himself to Dresden. The original manuscript, dated May 16, 1856, runs as follows :

MOST ILLUSTRIOUS KING AND LORD,

Relying on your Majesty's gracious indulgence, a man who from his former conduct must necessarily appear in the light of a criminal ventures to approach you with an attempted explanation of that conduct, in the hope that such a step may serve in a measure to support his most humble petition.

When, seven years ago, I resolved to take refuge in a foreign country rather than stand my trial on the charges brought against me, I was moved not so much by the fear of not obtaining a favourable verdict as by my despair of ever finding sufficient scope for the realization of my artistic ideals, even supposing I were fully reinstated in my former position. My previous experience had led me to take so gloomy a view of the future of art under the prevailing conditions that, after many fruitless attempts, I came at last to realize how impossible it was for me to obtain acceptance for my artistic views in Dresden. I saw, then, with ever greater clearness, that I should be compelled to break with these conditions—the conditions, be it noted, not the persons involved, as I had formerly imagined. To such a mood as this nothing was more calculated to give an erratic turn than the wild spirit of unrest which was at that time disturbing the world of politics. Though I never at any time attached myself to any particular party, nor had any sympathy with their specific theories and aspirations, still, a belief in a complete transformation of the political, and even more of the social, conditions gradually took so strong a hold on me that I began to indulge in visions of a new order of things in which my ideal of the proper relations of art to life might at last be realized.

Politics and the events of the day concerned me only in so far as I felt it my duty to try to bend my material aims to my artistic purposes ; but I never gave my serious support to any definitely political undertaking. However, I became in time so furious with the conditions under which I had to live that I lost my head completely and ended by regarding my personal position as no longer tenable. Whatever conclusion may have been drawn from my conduct during the Dresden riots—of which I had no previous knowledge—I was so little conscious of any criminal intention, least of all against my most gracious sovereign, that, when I was driven by stress of circumstances to fly the country, I was never clear as to the nature of the charge preferred against me. I soon learned that I was accused on all sides of the blackest ingratitude toward my exalted benefactor—this I can only regard as a tragic stroke of fate, the result of my imprudent behaviour in Dresden. The consequence is that I find myself branded with the stigma of a crime of which, though it seems impossible to disprove it, I must assert my innocence. So convinced was I of the hopelessness of clearing myself of such a charge that I decided to abandon the attempt so far as Dresden was concerned. This naturally implied a complete break with all that had gone before ; the only thing that sustained me in the painful situation was a truly morbid feeling of exaltation to which I gave myself over with a sort of desperate eagerness during the first years of my exile. With the desire of justifying my conduct I felt impelled to formulate, develop, and publish in a series of literary works these very theories about art and life which had brought about my downfall. These publications could not fail to give fresh offence, since they made it plain to all that my conduct, which had come to be regarded merely as that of a criminal, was actually the result of a philosophic system. But though my labours only made my position worse in the eyes of my judges, they had the good effect of cooling my excitement and gradually restoring me to mental health by the expulsion, as it were, of the peccant matter.

As time went on I found it possible once more to plan a work of pure art on the grand scale. As I applied myself to the task of execution, and so regained my artistic balance in the process, I experienced an inward change ; I began to have a deeper insight into the nature of things, which made me realize that my former views were mistaken. This is not the place to enlarge upon the nature of this revelation, nor of the confirmation which it received from external sources ; still, I venture to hope that your Majesty will find the solution in the humble petition I am about to make, in the promise which I consider myself bound to connect with it, and above all in the change which has taken place in myself.

I would cheerfully submit to my exile as the consequences of my former errors were it not that my art—at once the cause of these errors, the means of my purification, and my hope of forgiveness in the future—waves me back to my Fatherland. My art it is that binds me with indissoluble bonds to Germany, since only there can I hope to see my music dramas produced ; and that is an experience indispensable to the future progress of my art.

I may mention that, thanks to the especial favour of his Royal Highness the Grand Duke of Saxe-Weimar, as also to the generous interest of a friend of mine—himself a distinguished artist—a suitable retreat has been offered me in the town of Weimar, and it is my most earnest desire to be permitted to reside there for short periods from time to time. I therefore venture humbly to beseech your Majesty that you may be graciously pleased to consider my special quality and position as an artist, while passing over my conduct as a citizen and a subject, and to relax the regulations of the states of the German Confederation in my favour, so that it may be possible for me to proceed without let or hindrance to

Weimar, there to reside for such a period as may seem desirable.

In petitioning for this extraordinary favour I frankly and willingly acknowledge my grievous fault in deserting my proper sphere of art for the field of politics ; I also deeply and sincerely regret the fact that by such conduct I must have appeared guilty of the grossest ingratitude to my exalted benefactor, his lamented Majesty King Frederick Augustus. Though I cannot plead it in justification, it is nevertheless a consolation to me to know that I am innocent of this offence, and that it never occurred to me that my reckless action would be interpreted in this light. I pledge my word of honour that I will never again take part in any form of political activity, and in this connexion I am willing to submit myself to any reasonable form of surveillance. Finally, I undertake, when I return to Germany, carefully to avoid anything that might draw public attention to my personality in any way or in any place, as might very easily happen in the case of an artist whose works are fairly well known on the German stage.

I trust your Majesty will understand from what I have said that only an earnest desire for reconciliation, coupled with the wish to remove all hindrance to the further development of my art, emboldens me to appeal to your Majesty's clemency. May it be my good fortune to awaken a gracious and indulgent response in the heart of so enlightened a *connoisseur*, patron, and friend of the arts and sciences ! With deepest humility and devotion, I remain,

Your Majesty's most faithful subject,

RICHARD WAGNER

DRESDEN
May 16, 1856

Here, then, we have the full autograph text of the first confession of guilt, the first plea for forgiveness, that was wrung from Wagner after seven long years of bitter internal struggle. The document reached the

King on May 26 ; on June 2 his Majesty, after consulting with Zschinsky, the Minister of Justice, gave directions that it should be handed to the Ministry of Justice, and wrote to Zschinsky to that effect :

WESENSTEIN
June 2, 1856

DEAR FRIEND,

In accordance with your advice I have referred the matter of Wagner's petition to the Ministry of Justice, and I will ask you to instruct Hänel,[1] before any decision is given, to inform me further by word of mouth of the position of affairs.

Your devoted
JOHN

The petition reached the Ministry of Justice on June 4. To the credit of the Saxon authorities, as also of the King, it is to be noted that the appeal was not summarily rejected nor left to lie unread on the shelf. On the contrary, every effort was made to arrive at a clear idea of Wagner's actual share in the May revolution. There was no precise evidence against him on this head. As has been said before, no special proceedings had been taken against him in his absence ; but the *dossiers* of the guilty persons with whom Wagner was known to have had relations were now examined to see if there was any mention of Wagner's activities in the reports of those trials. As a result of these researches we have the first document in which the charges against Wagner are actually formulated (1854) ; its main points have been discussed in a previous passage of this work, where we dealt briefly with the question of Wagner's guilt.[2]

As might have been expected, the Ministry of

Justice decided to reject the appeal, but, in accordance with the King's desire, the decision had to be communicated to him by word of mouth. Consequently Privy Councillor August Otto Krug, in drawing up the reply, marked it as waiting to be signed by his Majesty, and the King's signature, " Jhs.," as well as the initials of the Minister (Dr Zschinsky), " D. Z.," actually appears in the rough draft ; so that the document may be said to express the King's intention also.

Here is the reply :

> To Herr Richard Wagner
> *Zürich*
>
> The petition presented by you to his Majesty the King on May 16 for the setting aside of the criminal proceedings instituted against you having, by his Majesty's desire, been handed to the Ministry of Justice, you are hereby informed that they are not inclined to recommend the granting of your suit.

After passing the Chancellor's office the decision was dispatched on August 11, the Ministry of Justice returned the incriminating document to the Dresden legal authorities, and, so far as the Saxon Government was concerned, the incident was closed. We do not know when the decision reached Wagner, nor how he received the news ; neither in his autobiography nor in his letters of that period is any mention made of this latest disappointment. That he had not been without hopes of success is plain from a passage in a letter from him to Liszt :

> My only interest in the result of my petition lies in the fact that, if it succeeds, I shall be free to come to you when I choose ; in that case you will probably have to put up with me for some time during the coming winter.

KING JOHN OF SAXONY

From a lithograph with the inscription, "Hanns Hanfstaengl fecit. Printed
by Fr. Hanfstaengl at Dresden."

Municipal Museum, Dresden   70

In a letter to Minna he speaks with still greater confidence. As he is expecting his amnesty, which will
enable him to visit Germany from time to time, especially in the winter session, he is thinking of moving
shortly to one of the Swiss summer resorts, Brunnen
perhaps, reserving just a *pied-à-terre* in Zürich. Wagner
was living at Mornex, near Geneva, at the time, for the
sake of the cure, which occupied him till the middle
of August. For weeks at a time the desire for Liszt's
company seems to have been uppermost in his thoughts,
though now Zürich, rather than Weimar, suggested
itself as the place of meeting. " If only you will come
to me here," he writes to his friend in July, " I shan't
bother about Saxony or Germany at all for a long time
to come." This letter shows no abandonment of hope
so far, but only a temporary postponement, and his
disappointment on receiving the news of failure, just
after his cure was finished, was probably all the more
bitter. However, the young Grand Duke of Weimar,
in spite of his rebuff from Dresden, again came forward
with fresh plans for his assistance, while Liszt's exertions on his friend's behalf never flagged. The Grand
Duke was all the more inclined to do something for
the composer after hearing from Liszt of the contents
of Wagner's letter to the King. He wrote at once
(August 21, 1856) to his Minister, von Watzdorf, saying
that, in his opinion, Wagner had now done all that was
possible, and that he intended to grant him permission
to come to Weimar for a fortnight in September, for
the purpose of hearing his own operas, though this
permission could not be repeated. Evidently Charles
Alexander by no means approved of John's direct

refusal, and was disposed, in spite of the latter's plain but friendly warning, to consult his own more generous instincts, as well as his taste for music. To this proposal von Watzdorf was obliged to offer an energetic protest; he did not shrink from reminding his master, though in the most delicate manner, that he was bound by the decision of the Diet of the Confederation, which did not allow special privileges to any individual sovereign of the confederacy. All through the Wagner affair, indeed, von Watzdorf, whose valuable services to the state of Saxe-Weimar are generally recognized, figures as a cool-headed statesman of King John's type, rather than as a warm-hearted, liberal-minded human being. Charles Alexander, however, was still determined to make one more effort on Wagner's behalf, and on October 21 he suggested that von Watzdorf should write to von Beust suggesting that he should procure a temporary revocation of the composer's exile. Von Watzdorf, however, absolutely refused to take action, and managed to put so bad a complexion on the affair that the Grand Duke was obliged to abandon his benevolent plans.

Wagner, who had heard, no doubt from Liszt, of what was going on, wrote to the Grand Duke on October 31 thanking him for all his sympathy and kindness. Whatever the result of his " magnanimous exertions " might be, he assures him of his grateful homage and unalterable devotion. But though he knew of the Duke's repeated efforts on his behalf, Wagner was ignorant of how these had been thwarted by the punctilious attitude of his Minister. This explains the fact that on Liszt's return to Weimar, after being with Wagner in Zürich and St Gallen from the middle of October to the end of November, he speaks several times in his letters of his ardent wish to join him soon. He even discusses the future in detail, debating whether he shall settle in Weimar or perhaps on the Altenburg; he would prefer to live *incognito*, though not without a certain amount of intercourse with the Court. Moreover, if Breitkopf and Härtel should still refuse to come to a satisfactory arrangement the Grand Duke can be relied upon for financial support.

The bitter reproaches which Wagner repeatedly brings against Charles Alexander for merely holding out hopes without fulfilling them cannot be justified, and in any case are much too harshly worded, though the composer, it is true, can never have known the full extent of the Grand Duke's efforts on his behalf as revealed in his correspondence with his leading Minister. In spite of his exalted position—or, rather, because of it—the Grand Duke was less free than any private citizen; in his letters to von Watzdorf we have clear proof again and again of his sincere desire to help Wagner, and if the results were not all that Wagner's optimistic fancy painted it was not the Grand Duke's fault.

In December 1856 Wagner was reminded with alarming suddenness of his awkward position, as a refugee liable to arrest, by a political disturbance which, like a bolt from the blue, set all Switzerland in a ferment —the abortive Neuenburg rising, which threatened to involve the peaceful republic of Switzerland, to which that principality properly belonged, in a war with the King of Prussia. Both sides began to arm, and it was

73

only by the intervention of Napoleon III and the conclusion of a treaty that a conflict was averted. Even as it was, Wagner dreaded the entrance of Prussian troops into Switzerland, and the consequent possibility of his arrest at the demand of Saxony or the German Diet. He begged Liszt to promise him letters of protection against any acts of violence on the part of Prussian troops; otherwise he would be compelled to fly to France for safety. Accordingly, Liszt himself wrote to Prince William,* not that he thought there was any real danger of war, but in order to interest the Prince generally in Wagner's favour. However, all such precautions turned out to be unnecessary.

Meanwhile Wagner's economic position was growing worse and worse. He had given up the annual payment which he had for years received from the German-Russian family of Ritter, and was now eagerly bent on obtaining some security for the future through the agency of the Grand Duke, to whom he offered his services for a fixed period every year after his readmission to Germany. Beyond this he had no expectations. " My amnesty," he writes to Liszt on January 6, 1857, " will only be granted when Saxony thinks proper: the authorities there are determined to assert their independence." Some light was thrown in the darkness, however, by Otto Wesendonk's generous offer of the " Asyl "—a country house on the Grüner Hügel, near Zürich, and close to the Wesendonk villa—at a low rental. In this way Wagner's long-cherished desire for a permanent place of residence was now satisfied. Relief from financial worries would now follow, as he

* Later William I, German Emperor.—TRANSLATOR.

believed, through the sale of *Der Ring* to Breitkopf and Härtel; the scores of *Das Rheingold* and *Die Walküre* were completed, and that of *Siegfried* was well advanced. All Liszt's efforts, however, failed to conquer that firm's hesitation to undertake so great a risk.

In the spring of 1857 Wagner, grotesquely enough, was called upon to give advice as to the flags proper to be displayed on the occasion of a visit by the King of Saxony. The proprietor of the Hotel Baur, where his Majesty put up when he came to Zürich, had written to the Wesendonks to inquire what were the Saxon colours. Mathilde Wesendonk applied to Wagner, who consented to supply the correct information, however ungraciously. He writes:

> To the father of my country I have nothing to say; should he have the effrontery to visit my humble cot, I shall show him the door. His colours are white and green, tell Baur!

His new house, and the completion of *Siegfried*, now kept him busily employed; yet, in spite of his satisfaction at being at last installed in a real home of his own, we find his thoughts turning again and again to his native land. Referring to a performance of *Lohengrin*, he writes:

> You never seem to think that I also should have liked to be present. Still, I respect the discreet silence which my high and mighty patrons so conscientiously maintain on the delicate subject of my return.

He then goes on to speak, half seriously, half in jest, of an invitation from the Emperor of Brazil to visit Rio de Janeiro.

IV

FURTHER ATTEMPTS FAIL

1857–58

The Intercession of the Grand Duke Frederick of Baden—Wagner's
Appeal to the Crown Prince Albert of Saxony.

THE year 1856 had been one of disappointment,
and although the spring of 1857 had cheered the
sorely tried Master with hopes of a permanent home of
his own, his constant longings and plans for a return
to Germany would not leave him in peace. However,
as soon as the faintest ray of light appeared on the
horizon he hailed it as a sure sign that the darkness was
soon to be lifted, and his sanguine expectations were
shortly to meet with fresh encouragement.

A daughter of the Princess Augusta of Prussia, the
young Princess Louise, who had long taken an interest
in Wagner's music, had, in 1856, become the wife of
the Grand Duke Frederick of Baden. Her interest
procured the performance of Wagner's operas in
Karlsruhe, and the composer wrote to thank her. The
Grand Duke replied in a friendly letter—" the first
sign," Wagner declared, " of a desire to break down
those barriers which suspicion, or Court etiquette, had
built up between us "—and expressed his willingness to
intervene in the matter of Wagner's repatriation. The
relations between the composer and the royal house of
Baden were strengthened by a visit to Zürich of the
Karlsruhe manager, Eduard Devrient, an intimate

acquaintance of Wagner in the old Dresden days, who held out hopes of a first performance of *Tristan* in Karlsruhe under his personal direction. No sooner, then, had his hopes of Weimar disappeared than further possibilities presented themselves in another place.

This friendly reception on the part of the Grand Duke emboldened the Master to beg him to intercede in his favour, so that no difficulties might be placed in his way by Saxony in the matter of his visit to Karlsruhe. After some delay, and more than one reminder on the part of Wagner, Frederick at last (November 27, 1857) decided to write himself to King John.

YOUR MAJESTY,

I am venturing to trouble you with these few lines in the hope of interesting you in a request the fulfilment of which would give me real pleasure. The operas of Richard Wagner are very popular in our theatre at the present time, and have been so well received as to warrant the revival of some of his earlier compositions. Wagner has repeatedly begged my permission to come to Karlsruhe, in order to hear his own operas, and I should certainly not hesitate to grant it if only he had obtained your Majesty's pardon. For that pardon I do not presume to appeal; I only desire that Wagner may have leave to live in Baden for a certain period, under strict supervision, and I am prepared to take every precaution to prevent him doing anything that might attract attention during his visit.

I beg, then, that your Majesty will authorize me to allow Richard Wagner to come here for about four weeks. I will guarantee that his stay shall not exceed that limit, and that he shall then leave Germany without delay.

Should your Majesty grant my request I shall always remain your debtor for such a mark of confidence, while at the same time your gracious act will give me special

pleasure, as I am convinced it will mean yet another important step in the development of our German art.
I remain, with sincere attachment and deep respect,
Your Majesty's faithful and devoted
FREDERICK, GRAND DUKE OF BADEN

KARLSRUHE
November 27, 1857

That the King would refuse the request was a foregone conclusion ; but as the Grand Duke of Baden, while not quite so close a connexion, ranked higher in importance than his cousin of Weimar, it was necessary that the refusal should be conveyed with the greater show of courtesy. Here is the King's answer :

I hasten to reply to your Royal Highness's valued communication of the 27th ult. with that frankness which is due to a Prince of the Federal States to whom I am bound by ties of kinship and amity.

The question whether Richard Wagner should be allowed to reside for a time in Karlsruhe is a matter which concerns your Royal Highness rather than myself, and I must therefore leave it entirely to your own judgment. If you decide in his favour I should not require any special police precaution, as I have no fear that Wagner will make any fresh attempt to disturb the peace of the German Federal States.

But if, as I understand you, your Royal Highness wishes me to proclaim a truce, as it were, with Wagner during his stay in Baden I greatly regret that I am unable to accede to your request, for reasons the justice of which I am sure you will recognize.

My lamented brother, it is true, was pleased to grant remission, complete or partial, of the sentences imposed on a large number of those concerned in the May revolution, as I too have done in not a few instances. At the same time it has been a rule with both of us to show no consideration to those fugitives who refuse to submit themselves to justice. In the case of Wagner it is all the more impossible to break this rule, from the fact that the man is unworthy of any consideration. Whether, if actually brought up for trial, he would be found guilty is uncertain, though circumstances are strongly against him and his notorious behaviour appears all the blacker when we remember that not only was he in the service of my late brother, but owed everything to him. When he came to Dresden, a poor man, unknown, and burdened with debts, my brother, recognizing his genius, gave him an excellent appointment, such as he was hardly entitled to expect. These benefactions Wagner repaid with base ingratitude ; he not only endeavoured to excite those under him to hostile demonstrations against the Government, but also—or so, at least, it is believed—took an active part in the traitorous attempts of May 1849. Your Royal Highness will therefore understand that, while something might be said for the other culprits, such a man as this deserves no more than the sternest justice. I may add that I have already had to refuse a precisely similar request with reference to Wagner from my cousin the Grand Duke of Weimar, and so cannot consistently alter my decision in the present case.

I trust your Royal Highness will pardon my frankness. I have thought it right to acquaint you with certain circumstances of which you were probably unaware, and although my decision may be a disappointment to you, I hope that, after weighing the reasons that have dictated it, you will not allow it to interfere with our present friendly relations.

Your Royal Highness's most devoted

JOHN, KING OF SAXONY

DRESDEN
December 2, 1857

Here again, as in the case of the Weimar petition, we have a flat refusal, though in one place perhaps we may detect a slightly less uncompromising disposition. In shifting the responsibility for Wagner's visit to the Grand Duke's shoulders the King explains that the police regulations will not be insisted on, though he qualifies the statement by adding that this must not be interpreted as meaning that Saxony was prepared to renounce its right to bring Wagner to justice. Such a concession would have been looked upon almost as an abandonment of any further criminal proceedings, a possibility which John wished to avoid on strictly legal grounds, in view of the severity with which the other culprits had been treated.

Such, then, was the result of the Baden intercession. With this extinction of his latest hopes Wagner was once more compelled to realize that Saxony was the actual arbiter of his destiny. No personal goodwill on the part of individual princes could remove the obstacle presented by the irreconcilable attitude of Dresden toward the political offenders. In spite, then, of his repeated declarations that he would have nothing more to do with Saxony, bitter necessity compelled Wagner once again to turn his thoughts in that direction. Fairly resigned to his fate, he writes to Fischer on October 29, 1857 :

> I still see little to hope for from Dresden, where the King is said to be very ill-disposed toward me—though I can hardly believe that the good folks of the town still remember my foolish escapades of nine years ago. However, God's will be done ! Even though I never get my amnesty, I must console myself with the thought that, after all, I should not be likely to derive much pleasure from the German theatres.

Wagner, it is true, had retired from active politics immediately after his flight ; but to refer to his former political activities as merely " foolish escapades " seems rather surprising.

Soon after this, in the month of November, he seems to have contemplated a new step toward reconciliation. He sent Fischer certain definite proposals, to be communicated to the General Manager von Lüttichau, for a settlement (assuming an amnesty) of the floating debt he had contracted with the Dresden Theatrical Pension Fund in 1848. Fischer, however, replied that he had done nothing in the matter, because, first, he was not certain if the debt still existed, and, secondly, he was convinced that there was no likelihood of an amnesty. Wagner replied (December 2, 1857) begging his friend to say nothing to von Lüttichau,

> for, I assure you, the only thing which could induce me to make a further appeal to the Court of Dresden is the thought of the difficult position in which I should be placed should a settlement of the debt be demanded. Besides, my strongest desire now is to remain a free man, and never again to enter into any sort of engagement; the very mention of Dresden, the theatre, Lüttichau, etc., awakens such painful recollections that I like to think I have done with them for ever.

He goes on to tell him that the Grand Duke of Baden had informed him of his letter to the King of Saxony; he does not know if anything has come of it, but fears not; however, he has made the above inquiries in case his affairs should be brought up once more before the Dresden authorities.

The beginning of 1858, as we have seen, brought no change in his political outlook, although twelve months before he had been confident that the coming year would see the end of his exile. Now, on February 7, 1858, he writes to Fischer, " Heavens ! Who would have thought it possible that nine years would pass and still no sign of an amnesty!" But while he could write thus, he was busily at work in a new direction.

The King's eldest son, the Crown Prince Albert, whose marriage five years before had given rise to hopes of a general pardon, was a great lover of music and a keen pianist, having been a pupil of the once-esteemed teacher and Court pianist, Karl Krägen. As he was familiar with Wagner's music, the Master could the more confidently rely on his assistance, since it was precisely on musical grounds that Wagner's appeals for repatriation were chiefly based—he hoped to use the son's interest in music and his goodwill toward the composer as keys to the heart of the royal parent.

Wagner, however, did not venture to address a letter [1] directly to Albert, but sent it (February 19) to his old friend Fischer, with a request that he would

> deliver it without delay, either personally or through the agency of Heine, or any well-disposed and influential person, into the hands of the addressee. It is of no use to pretend any longer, unless I see a speedy likelihood of procuring an amnesty, I am finished; either I must be allowed the refreshment of conducting my own works or I shall give up the struggle once for all!

The letter is as follows :

YOUR ROYAL HIGHNESS,
The memory of the benevolent interest you were once pleased to show in my works encourages me in the request I am about to make, that your Royal Highness would deign to intercede with his Majesty the King, your exalted father, with a view to relieving my unfortunate position.

Two years have passed since I ventured to approach his Majesty with a petition that he might be graciously

THE CROWN PRINCE ALBERT OF SAXONY

From a lithograph with the inscription, "Hanns Hanfstaengl, 1854. Printed by
Fr. Hanfstaengl in Dresden." 82

pleased to quash the proceedings begun against me on account of my share in the unhappy disturbances of 1849. That petition contained a frank description of the extraordinary mental process through which I have passed, and which, owing to the hindrances that barred the way to the goal of my ideals, led me into the error of supposing that a complete change of the political and social conditions of mankind might serve as a foundation for a noble development of the arts in public life and their relations to humanity at large.

I came to recognize that, in the *exalté* mood in which I then found myself, I must have laid myself open to the charge, if not of deliberately treasonable conduct, at least of a recklessness in my personal behaviour which, in conjunction with the compromising nature of my associates, might well assume a criminal aspect. My gradual emancipation from this morbid state of mind, my complete absorption once more in my art, together with the desire to be allowed to practise it without further hindrance—these, as I stated, were the grounds of my petition, and my reasons for hoping that his Majesty might be graciously pleased to pardon an erring man.

The answer to my petition was a brief note from the Royal Minister of Justice to the effect that it had been handed to him by his Majesty for consideration, but had failed to meet with a favourable reception. Great as was my disappointment, I had to acknowledge the strict justice, under the exceptional circumstances, of the decision.

Since then two years have gone by. The hope I entertained of a favourable turn in my affairs, fostered as it was by the kind sympathy and personal advocacy of their Royal Highnesses the Grand Dukes of Saxe-Weimar and Baden, have not been fulfilled, and with the lapse of time my general circumstances have become so straitened as to be no longer tolerable, and incompatible with any further artistic endeavour. If I venture now to approach your Royal Highness it is in a last desperate effort to ensure the possibility of continuing my work as a composer, on which my very existence depends. Since strict justice is bound to reject my petition, I throw myself once more at the feet of mercy, and appeal in the last resort to the heart of your Royal Highness, the worthy son of my supreme judge.

I am well aware that in suggesting that your Royal Highness should recommend the granting of an amnesty I am doing something exceptional or scarcely permissible ; but I may be allowed to point out that my case itself is exceptional in every way. Ought I really to be regarded only, or primarily, as a political offender ? Is it fair that the overwrought mood of an optimistic dreamer who lives only in his art should be judged with the same severity as the ambitious plottings of a political fanatic ? As a matter of fact, the sympathy shown me by the illustrious Princes mentioned above proves, to my consolation, that they had recognized the difference in the two cases and given the verdict in my favour. Now that I stand before the supreme judge of the land, in whose sight I must certainly seem worthy of a severe sentence, I still cherish a hope that even here, when the fault has been confessed and repented of, the culprit may be regarded with a lenient eye ; it is because I feel the weakness of my defence that I turn for mercy not to the Royal Courts of Justice, but to the gracious clemency of my most illustrious sovereign, and beseech him to decide between the claims of outraged justice and an artist's need for protection.

I trust your Royal Highness will allow me to set forth in a few words the situation from which I crave deliverance.

No composer was ever so dependent as I upon the support of those who speak his native tongue. I have never been able to compose except to my own text— both words and music are firmly rooted, in a manner unprecedented, in the German language and the German spirit ; hence my struggles, ever since my exile, to find a new home for myself on foreign soil have been without success—even in Paris, a city to which, in other respects, I felt most strongly attracted. In my present place of retirement, German Switzerland, the theatres are so entirely inadequate that I find it impossible to make any use of them; consequently I have now spent nine years in exile without being able even to contemplate any performance of my own works. I have not yet been able to produce my opera *Lohengrin*, written when I was still in Dresden, to say nothing of any of my later works. On my shelves lie three new scores, *Das Rheingold, Die Walküre, Der junge Siegfried*, to remind me with their " poor dumb mouths " of the sad plight in which I find myself. Yet so completely does my life depend upon the exercise of my art that I am at present engaged on a new dramatic composition; but so broken is my heart with grief and misery, so crippled and hampered is my spirit by the desolating thought that this work also must remain unproduced, that I feel my strength is giving way. To these mental sufferings must be added the distress occasioned by acute financial difficulties; I am without means of any kind, the sums received for my earlier works are nearly exhausted, and my only chance of making any more money is by the successful production of a new work. Still, however desperate my situation, I could never bring myself to consent to the first performance of a new work of mine unless I myself were present; it is essential that the composer should assist in the preliminary study of his work, and be present at rehearsals —only with these are his labours ended. In this connexion my own sensibilities have been so frequently outraged by unhappy experience that I should prefer that my works should remain unheard rather than forgo my necessary share in the final stages of production. The thought of all this plunges me into the profoundest melancholy, which, for the sake of others, I must try to conceal; the result is that I have taken to brooding in solitude until all my natural cheerfulness has forsaken me and I am weary of my life.

This, your Royal Highness, is a just description of my situation—though I have suppressed many a bitter, painful detail—deliverance from which depends entirely on my being permitted to enter Germany once more without let or hindrance. My object in wishing to return is certainly not to enjoy such empty triumphs as might easily be won by an artist whose works have met with applause in many theatres ; my sole desire is to be able to be present now and again at the rehearsals and performances of my works, especially the later ones, by competent artists in a properly equipped theatre. Moreover, I have, strangely enough, such a real dislike of public demonstrations that I should find it no hardship to pledge my word never to come into personal contact with the public, except at the desire, and with the express permission, of the Court. I am prepared to give any guarantee of good behaviour that may be required of me from whatever quarter, and I am quite willing to submit to any form of supervision that may be thought necessary, so long as it does not interfere with the main purpose of my return to Germany.

Should your Royal Highness consider it worth while to forward my suit with his Majesty the King, setting forth my object and the conditions I am prepared to accept, I should look upon this as my last chance of rehabilitating myself as both artist and man. I will not venture to speak of gratitude to your Royal Highness, since, alas, the most distressing result of my former error is the charge of ingratitude to which I inevitably laid myself open. But if the sincere endeavours of one who has been purged by heavy suffering can do aught to merit forgiveness I swear from the bottom of my heart to be always mindful of your gracious kindness. And, however the world may censure the passionate and irritable character of an artist like myself, I may still hope that your Royal Highness, when once you are acquainted with my compositions as a whole, will acknowledge that I have always endeavoured to depict what is noble and sublime, and that if a man of this type can for a moment seem base and ignoble it is merely the result of a passing cloud of error.

If in dealing with my unhappy situation I have ventured to advance certain facts which put my conduct in a favourable light I trust your Royal Highness will pardon my freedom and my bluntness of speech in consideration of my heavy affliction, and will allow me to conclude by offering my most sincere and heartfelt wishes for your health and happiness.

Your Royal Highness's most humble servant,

RICHARD WAGNER

ZÜRICH
February 20, 1858

It was the custom for the Ministry of Justice to send a reply, were it only in the form of a curt refusal, to all petitions addressed to the King; but in this case no answer seems to have been sent. None, at least, passed through the ordinary channels, and the original letter shows no sign of any official stamp : it seems to have been treated as a private communication which the Prince merely discussed with his royal father. Whatever John's answer may have been, the result was silence. Although Liszt had hinted on May 7 that little was to be hoped for just then from Dresden, but that he would himself once more approach the Grand Duke of Baden on the subject of the proposed residence in Karlsruhe, it was months apparently before Wagner himself gave up all hope ; in letters written in May and June he constantly speaks of the amnesty which he is expecting, even though it may be delayed for some time.

A revival of his operas in Dresden, with Tichatschek as a special attraction, seemed to promise well and raised Wagner's hopes still higher. On June 20 he wrote to Minna, " They are going to do my *Rienzi* in Dresden after all. . . . This revival of my operas is a very good sign and must undoubtedly help to further the cause of my amnesty."

87

Rienzi was successfully performed on August 25, 1858, with Tichatschek in the title-*rôle*. It would seem that the Crown Prince's enthusiasm for Wagner's music had at least achieved a preliminary success in restoring the composer's works, though not the composer himself, to the original home from which, many years ago, they had started on their career. This time it was not merely a case of the chance revival of a single work ; Wagner's other operas (*Tannhäuser*, for instance, with Wagner's niece Johanna as Elizabeth) were once more welcome at the Dresden Court Theatre, and on August 6, 1859, *Lohengrin* was given in Semper's new opera-house, with Tichatschek as the hero.

On July 23 and 24 a meeting took place at Lucerne between Wagner and his Weimar supporters, at the invitation of the Grand Duke, who had himself selected the place as one where he could appear in the capacity of art-patron rather than as Prince and a member of the German Confederation, and so feel himself free to act without regard for Dresden. The conversations were of the friendliest nature ; the Grand Duke was most cordial in his expressions of the interest he felt in Wagner's compositions, and the Grand Duchess was not less gracious ; but on the question of Wagner's return to Germany the meeting failed to produce any tangible results.

Disappointed in this direction, Wagner began to build ever stronger hopes (during the years 1858 and 1859) on the assistance of the Grand Duke of Baden, who, he imagined, would procure his temporary return to Germany for the rehearsals of *Tristan*, in order that Karlsruhe might have the honour of the first production of that opera. So great was his confidence on this head that on October 19, 1858, he assured the Darmstadt conductor, Schindelmeisser, that the Grand Duke of Baden had actually obtained the King of Saxony's permission for him to visit a certain German town at a given time, in order to superintend the production of a new work. Darmstadt, he added, should have the second claim to consideration.

About this time, too, a new star of hope seemed to be rising in another quarter. A paragraph went the round of the German newspapers which, however surprising, certainly pointed to a new and powerful supporter of Wagner's interests. On June 28, 1858, he writes to Minna :

> You will see from the enclosed that the Emperor of Austria is reported to have spoken for me at the Court of Dresden. This may well be; if it is true, I owe it to the Grand Duke of Weimar, who was in Vienna a short time ago and must have urged the Emperor to act. The paragraph also shows quite clearly King John's view of the situation. Does he really suppose that I shall consent first of all to be tried and sentenced in Dresden ?[1] However, it is certain that matters must now come to a crisis.

What the actual enclosure was is not known, but we may suppose it was similar to the paragraph which appeared in the *Dresdener Volkszeitung* for June 28, 1858.

The *Frankfurter Journal* contains the following news from Dresden (June 22) :

> The case of Richard Wagner has been a favourite topic of conversation of late in almost every circle. It is said not only that two Thuringian princes have interested themselves in his behalf, but that similar action has also

been taken in the highest quarters at Vienna. The Government of Saxony, however, still refuses to depart from the conditions laid down as the result of the May rebellion—*i.e.*, Wagner must first submit himself to the proper authorities and let the law take its course before there can be any question of pardon.

Possibly Wagner saw the actual item in the *Frankfurter Journal*, or something similar in another paper, and may have interpreted "the highest quarters at Vienna" as meaning the Emperor himself. The paragraph was, in fact, a mixture of truth and falsehood. Nothing is known of any intervention by the Emperor Francis Joseph. Of his letters to King John, preserved in the domestic archives at Dresden, not one has any reference to Wagner, and it would be strange indeed if such a letter were missing while the petitions of the Grand Dukes of Baden and Weimar have been preserved. On the other hand, the reference to the demands of Saxony that Wagner should stand his trial is strictly accurate; this condition is mentioned by King John in his letter to the Grand Duke of Baden, and in the Ministry of Justice's reply to Minna's petition in 1854 it is expressly stated that only on such terms could the question of pardon be considered.

V

WAGNER IN VENICE
1858–59

Wagner's Petitions to the General Manager, von Lüttichau, and
the Minister of Justice, von Behr.

IN the spring of 1858 Wagner received a blow that
struck home. Owing to Minna's not altogether
groundless jealousy of Mathilde Wesendonk and her
uncivil behaviour to that lady, the intimate relations
existing between the two families were broken off, and
Wagner was obliged to give up the "Asyl," the country
house near Zürich which Herr Wesendonk had placed
at his disposal. Quick to see the necessity for a temporary separation, Wagner sent his wife to take the cure
at Brestenburg on the Hallwyler See, where she might
face her troubles in peaceful solitude. When in July
Minna, who was not remarkable for delicacy of feeling,
returned to her husband he soon realized the impossibility of remaining any longer in the old familiar neighbourhood. Accordingly he began to look about for
some temporary residence in a healthy locality, where
he might work in peace and without fear of disturbance.

Germany was given up as hopeless; Austria too,
as part of the German Confederation. England had
failed to please him on his visit in 1855. He had never
felt at home in France; even Paris, the only city that
held out any inducements to an artist, had no charms
for him. Italy was the only country left. In a letter

to Minna on August 19 he cannot make up his mind—
he is afraid of the heat in a southern clime.   On August
25 he seems inclined to accept the proposal of his young
friend Karl Ritter that he should give Venice a trial ;
the quiet of the streets attracted him.   Indeed, his only
reason for hesitating was that Venice at the time
belonged to the Austrian Empire.[1]   True, it was not
part of the German Confederation, and the warrant for
his arrest by the German police could not reach him
there ; but he was not quite certain as to the attitude
of the Austrian Government—he might possibly be
expelled from the city.   In a letter to Liszt (August 20)
he asked him to find out whether it would be possible
for him to reside in Venice for a time without being
molested ; in case of difficulty Liszt was to ask the
Grand Duke of Weimar to use his influence as a friend.
The doubtful tone of Liszt's reply induced Wagner to
make direct inquiries, through a friend, at the Austrian
Embassy in Berne.   The Ambassador in his answer
(August 24), while not absolutely pledging himself,
gave it as his opinion that Wagner need have no anxiety
with regard to the Austrian passport ; whereupon the
composer wrote at once to Liszt, laying stress on the
necessity of choosing a restful place and the special
claims of Venice in this respect.   Consequently the
Grand Duke was to do his best to ensure the possibility
of a long stay in that city.   Liszt replied (August 26) on
behalf of the Grand Duke, advising Genoa or Sardinia
in preference to Venice, but the advice arrived too late,
as Wagner had already started that very day on his
journey.   He arrived in Venice on the 29th, and found
apartments in the Palazzo Giustiniani on the Grand

THE PALAZZO GIUSTINIANI, WAGNER'S HOME IN VENICE
From a view of part of the Grand Canal.   92

Canal, which combined internal quiet with a view of the ever-changing scene outside.[1]

No difficulties were put in his way at first, though it is noticeable that the various police authorities adopted quite different and individual attitudes toward him. The Ambassador in Berne had viséd his passport without hesitation; the Prime Minister and Secretary for Foreign Affairs, Count von Buol-Schauenstein,[2] maintained a discreet and dignified calm; while the Chief of the Police, Baron Kempen von Fichtenstamm,[3] appears in the *rôle* of sinister bureaucrat and republican-hunter. The Venetian officials, meanwhile, were not merely correct and courteous, but even benevolent, in spite of Kempen's orders. That gentleman, who had somehow got wind of Wagner's movements, lost no time in sending a telegram in cipher to Venice (September 3): " The Saxon refugee Richard Wagner, author and composer, is said to be in Venice. If this is so how did he get permission to travel, and what is his motive ? "

The next day a reply was sent by telegram that Wagner had arrived from Zürich on August 30 with a Swiss passport; he was in very bad health, and would remain for six months or a year; Wagner was living in retirement, and expecting a visit shortly from the celebrated Liszt. No sooner did this information reach Vienna (September 5) than Kempen, in his own peculiar fashion, communicated it to the Secretary for Foreign Affairs, with the following comment:

Richard Wagner, as is well known, was one of the leaders in the May revolution in Saxony; apart from general political objections to the presence of such a

93

person in any part of the Imperial dominions, the Saxon Government is hardly likely to be pleased at finding him tolerated in Austria.

Kempen, therefore, would be glad of von Buol's opinion as to what proceedings should be taken against Wagner, " in view of the consideration due to the Saxon Government."

This display of narrow-minded self-importance on the part of the police magnate, however, was little to the taste of the responsible statesman. In his reply (September 10) Buol leaves to Kempen's own discretion the question of the political undesirability of Wagner's residence within the Empire, but dismisses the diplomatic aspect of affairs with cold politeness. The idea of giving any special consideration to a second-rate state like Saxony was naturally painful to the representative of a Great Power such as Austria. He writes :

> With regard to any possible annoyance to Saxony, I have so far received no representations from them which would warrant such a conclusion, and am therefore not entitled to object to Wagner's presence in Austrian territory on political grounds. It might even be that the Saxon Government, so far as it is still interested in the doings of Wagner, would prefer that he should reside in Austria, where he would be under strict police supervision, rather than in Switzerland, where no such control is possible. Meanwhile, should your Excellency think it important for your own guidance to learn the wishes of the Saxon Government on this matter, I should be very pleased to address a confidential inquiry to Dresden in accordance with any suggestion your Excellency may be pleased to make.

Kempen, as one might suppose, was not particularly pleased at this rebuff ; in his reply (September 12) he suggested that Saxony, while suffering Wagner to remain under the protection of the Imperial Government, might well feel uneasy, and at the same time not see its way to taking the initiative in the matter. Since, however, the Minister did not consider it desirable that the first step should come from Austria, he (Kempen) would leave all further action to the enlightened discretion of his Excellency. In spite, however, of his dislike of any improper interference on the part of the police, Buol observed the conventional forms of diplomacy so far as to instruct (September 20) the Austrian *chargé d'affaires* in Dresden, Count Hugo Traun-Abensberg,[1] to inform the Saxon Government officially that Wagner had arrived at Venice on August 30 with a Swiss passport; that he was there for his health, and had made arrangements for a stay of six months or perhaps even longer. During his visit he would naturally be kept under supervision by the Imperial police.

This was just a brief diplomatic note, without reference to any special wishes on the part of Saxony. The position, however, was perfectly correct; the official tone of friendliness was preserved, while at the same time Austria gave up none of her sovereign rights in Venice, which did not belong to the Confederation. Accordingly Saxony had to rest content with Traun's pronouncement; on September 24 the Foreign Office communicated the Austrian Note to the Ministry of Justice, as well as to the Home Office. On September 30 the Minister of Justice, Zschinsky, laid the matter before the King; and, with the endorsement " To be dealt with as occasion requires," the affair was at an end.

But let us turn from Vienna and Dresden to Venice. The police authorities in that city were naturally not satisfied with the short telegraphic message of September 3 mentioned above ; on the very next day they had drawn up a detailed report of Wagner's situation and proceedings in Venice for Kempen's benefit. The writer of this document, Police Councillor Crespi, or the subordinate who supplied him with the materials, must have been a lover of music and a person of intelligence who was interested in the new Wagnerian movement. So favourable indeed is the report that one has the feeling that the police were prepared to do their best to remove all obstacles from the composer's path. Crespi writes as follows : [1]

VENICE
September 5, 1858

Richard Wagner, Kapellmeister to the Court of Dresden up to May 1849, is known to have been concerned to a certain extent in the disturbances of that time and in consequence was forbidden to return to Saxony. Since then his home has been in Switzerland—mostly in Zürich —where he has abstained from all political activities and devoted himself exclusively to his profession, in which as composer, musical essayist, and critic he has shown genius of a high and original order ; as the begetter of the so-called " music of the future " he stands at the head of the musical and æsthetic movements of the day. His operas —*e.g.*, his *Lohengrin,* which was given a few days ago at the Court Theatre in Vienna with the greatest success— have gradually won permanent favour in most of the Court Theatres of Germany, and have brought the composer countless testimonies of appreciation.

For some years his physicians have strongly recommended him to try a change to some southern climate, but he has been too occupied with composition to follow their advice. When it became evident, however, that

96

there was danger in further delay he at last decided to make a long stay in Venice, where he is now living quietly and in retirement.

As a proof of the overwrought state of his nerves we may mention that on the day of his arrival at the Palazzo Giustiniani he asked his landlord's permission to change the wallpaper of his apartment, which was too red for his taste, and the very next day he had the rooms repapered. Furthermore, he has ordered the servants to admit no one—even distinguished visitors are said to have been turned away. Although, as the central figure of the new musical movement, Wagner must naturally have an exceptionally extensive correspondence, the fact that he actually receives very few letters at the present time leads one to suppose that he has arranged for the restriction of their delivery in order to avoid any unnecessary mental strain.

Wagner's Zürich passport is dated July 29 of this year—No. 724.

CRESPI

If the object of this letter was to influence the police authorities at headquarters in Vienna in favour of the man who was implicated in the May rebellion it was based on a complete miscalculation. His Excellency Baron von Kempen was a thoroughgoing reactionary in all matters pertaining to the maintenance of public order, and was not the man to let his most sacred convictions be shaken by the mere opinion of a credulous subordinate. He lost no time in dispatching a fairly sharp note of admonition to the (in his opinion) too confiding headquarters at Venice :

VIENNA
September 9, 1858

To the Chief of the Police in Venice [1]

In your report of the 5th inst. dealing with the refugee Wagner, far too little importance is attached to the political aspect of the case. Wagner's movements at the time of the May revolution were in the highest degree compromising, and his subsequent association with the directors of revolutionary propaganda during his stay in Zürich was not calculated to allay the suspicions attaching to him. I must therefore request you to keep the political suspect in question under the strictest supervision during his stay in Venice, and to inform me without delay of anything noteworthy in his behaviour. At the same time you will have the goodness to report to me—as you should have done in the first place—which are the police authorities that have endorsed Wagner's passport from Zürich. This must be attended to without delay.

However much Franceschinis, as Chief of the Police, may have felt the reproach conveyed in this note, Wagner at any rate was not affected by it : the local authorities left him in peace. It is true they required his passport for further inspection, but they returned it to him with the assurance that no objection would be raised against his stay in Venice. The fact that their note was addressed to " the celebrated Herr Richard Wagner " evidently gratified his vanity, as we gather from his letter to Minna of September 28. This courteous treatment was doubtless due to the music-loving Crespi, to whom also fell the duty of replying (September 18) to the ungracious note from Vienna. After a few words as to the " most careful and discreet watch " that had been kept over Wagner's movements it continues :

> After further investigation I can only conclude that Wagner's reasons for coming to Venice are the state of his health and the hope that the mild climate will be good for his nervous attacks. His proceedings so far have borne out this view. He lives in retirement and sees scarcely anyone ; he has paid but one visit to the theatre

—the Camploy Theatre at San Samuele, for Ristori's *début* in *Maria Stuart* last week ; and this evening, at the pressing invitation of his landlord, he is going to the Gallo Theatre at San Benedetto to hear *Semiramide*. I may add that when yesterday the well-known Count von Gallenberg,[1] who had just arrived on the Lloyd steamer *Jupiter* with the members of the German Railway Congress, expressed his desire to visit Wagner the composer declined the honour.

The passport, it appears, was issued by the Swiss Confederacy (No. 724) on July 29, 1859, for Austria and Italy; it was viséd in Berne on July 30 for the Imperial States, and at Sesto Calende on August 28 by the customs.

Still the Chief of Police at Vienna was not satisfied. On October 1 a further message was dispatched to Venice, this time not to the police authorities, but to the council presided over by the Governor, Count von Bissingen-Nippenburg.[2] After a few preliminary remarks on Wagner's visit Kempen proceeds :

> There is no getting away from the fact that the granting of this passport has opened the door to an individual whose presence in any part of the Austrian Empire is thoroughly disagreeable, both from our own political point of view and also for its possible effect upon a friendly Government like Saxony. Still, however much we may desire to get rid of a man like Wagner—and in view of his antecedents I find it hard to believe that his health is the sole reason for his visit—I will refrain at present, through considerations of humanity, from issuing any special orders that might hinder his stay in Venice. Nevertheless, I would suggest, in a friendly spirit, that, as Wagner must not be permitted to settle in any other part of the Empire, the best plan would be to give definite orders to the police to keep a careful eye on the state of his health and, so soon as an improvement sets in, to take the proper

steps to procure his departure from Venice and from Austrian territory altogether.

Kempen sent a copy of this document at the same time to Count von Buol, though taking care to omit the reference to the blame assigned to the Berne Embassy.

This put an end for the time to the painful question of Wagner's residence in Venice, and the Master was now free to give his whole attention to his health and the composition of *Tristan*, undisturbed, with very few exceptions, by troublesome visitors and the claims of society.

On one point the police reports were intentionally silent—the friendly relations between Wagner and the Austrian military, which would certainly have filled Lieutenant-General Kempen with the darkest suspicions. The bands of the regiments stationed in Venice were in the habit of playing extracts from Wagner's operas, and they eagerly sought the composer's advice, while the officers welcomed his appearance in barracks with every sign of respect. Tiresome as such demonstrations generally were to him, he was obviously delighted in this case, as we see from his lively account in a letter to Minna dated October 28.

While Wagner was occupied with scoring Act II of *Tristan* his friend Liszt was engaged at home in trying to move the Grand Dukes of Weimar and Baden to fresh efforts on his behalf.[1] Wagner, however, with his variable temperament, the perpetual ebb and flow of his opinions, feelings, hopes, and desires, made it rather difficult for his friends; even Liszt's patience and consideration were often sorely tried by the irritable mood of his friend Richard. One day lauded to the skies, scolded the next for not doing enough for his friend, Liszt never failed him ; only now and then, when Wagner's proposals or demands became fantastically impossible, would he give a quiet refusal in terms well calculated not to give offence. Although for the last three years Wagner had been clamouring feverishly for an amnesty, loudly protesting that without it his entire life's work would be wasted,[1] a letter to Liszt, of January 2, 1859, points to a complete change of mind.

> After ten years of exile I have got so accustomed to it that I regard the question of an amnesty as of less import-ance than the certainty of a comfortable, care-free exist-ence for the rest of my life. A return to Germany would be merely a relative advantage ; the only positive gain would be the enjoyment of your society. The projected performance of my operas, even with my assistance, would mean little more than toil, trouble, and vexation. . . . Consequently, I have come to the conclusion that, so long as *Tristan* remains uncompleted, an amnesty would only place me in an awkward position. . . . Any scheme for assuring me a reasonable existence would be futile if dependent merely on the amnesty and coupled with the discharge of certain regular services : I cannot and I will not accept what is called an appointment, or anything of a similar nature. What I require is the definite assurance of an honourable and ample allowance, simply and solely for the purpose of enabling me to continue my work as composer undisturbed, and quite independent of any out-side considerations.

A royal coalition, it seems, was to find the necessary funds ; Liszt was to prepare the way by sounding the Grand Duke of Weimar, or, if Liszt thought best, Wagner would write direct to his Royal Highness ; failing this, they must try the Grand Duke of Baden.

This letter, it will be noticed, is more exacting in its

demands than the one written on a former occasion with a similar purpose. At that time Wagner was willing to give his services in return for the promised support, but in the present instance we are struck by his high estimate of his own value, the proud self-sufficiency which makes him reject even such a position as Liszt himself was content to fill in Weimar. Yet, though we may wonder at, and even blame, such an attitude, in view of his straitened circumstances and the fact that he owed his very existence to the extraordinary generosity of his friends, we cannot withhold our admiration from his unshakable belief in himself and his real value.

A large part of the musical public was still ignorant or suspicious of his works, and the majority of his professional colleagues regarded him with coldness or hostility. While we may well apply to Wagner the first half of the well-known quotation from Schiller, " Leicht bei einander wohnen die Gedanken," * Liszt, who, great artist as he was, never once lost touch with actualities, must have felt the truth of the antithesis, " Doch hart im Raume stossen sich die Sachen." † Indeed, his friend's ideas and visions could not be realized so lightly.

Before Liszt had time to reply Wagner wrote again, on January 7, to cancel his letter of January 2. The letter on which only five days before his very fate depended was now to be regarded as having never existed! However, the letters which follow tell a different tale, and on February 25 we find a consider-

* " Most varied thoughts may dwell in peace together."
† " But sharp's the tussle when they come to action."

Franz Liszt

From Ernst Rietschel's original model in plaster in the collection of sculpture at Dresden.
(The copy in marble is in the Liszt Museum at Weimar.)

able change of disposition. Even earlier, on February 9, he had written a letter to von Lüttichau in which he disowned every principle and resolve which at the beginning of the year he had so firmly upheld. However, before we turn our attention to that matter we must first give a glance at the position of affairs in Saxony.

After Wagner's departure for Venice Minna had given up housekeeping; and at the beginning of September 1858 she left Switzerland and returned to Saxony, in order to make a new home in Dresden in accordance with her husband's wishes, so that later, when Germany was once more open to him, he might have a *pied-à-terre*, a place to rest in. He writes to Minna on September 28 that he is very glad she has decided to settle in Dresden. "Yesterday," he says, "I wrote to Tichatschek about it. After all, Dresden is the only town where I can really feel at home—all other places seem like foreign countries." [1]

At first it seems as if there might be some difficulty with the police over the question of residence, and Wagner raged with his customary fury against Dresden and the Dresdeners. However, all was soon settled satisfactorily. Soon after her arrival Minna had called on Manager von Lüttichau, from whom she met with a cordial reception; she must have acted (as we gather from her husband's expressions of surprise) on her own initiative, just as she had done in the matter of her petition to the King in 1854. This gracious behaviour on the part of his former chief was not without its effect upon Wagner, who was now prepared to regard the much-abused von Lüttichau in a friendlier light;

and when he heard, further, that Minna was doing her utmost to forward his interests, and even cultivating the acquaintance of influential personages who might be useful in the future in the matter of the amnesty, Wagner concluded that the time had come for him to make some new effort on his own behalf. The low state of his finances at the beginning of the year, the failure, or his own voluntary abandonment, of the sanguine schemes he had outlined in his letter to Liszt of January 2, 1859—these things may have urged him to write the long letter to von Lüttichau which we shall now give : [1]

VENICE
February 9, 1859

YOUR EXCELLENCY,

The time has come when it is absolutely necessary that I should know definitely where I stand and what the future has in store for me ; whether I am ever to be allowed to return to Germany, or whether I must renounce that hope once for all, and look, for the future, to foreign countries for my means of livelihood as well as the opportunity for carrying out my artistic undertakings.

Your Excellency is probably aware that, some time ago, first the Grand Duke of Saxe-Weimar and, later, the Grand Duke of Baden made strong representations to his Majesty the King of Saxony, in favour of my return to Germany. Three years ago I myself approached his Majesty directly with an appeal for an amnesty, and a year ago made earnest entreaty to his Royal Highness Prince Albert to intercede on my behalf. To all these applications I have received no answer.[2] Moreover, judging from the measures lately taken by the Government of Saxony to induce the Imperial Government of Austria to put an end to my residence in Venice, I must conclude, to my sorrow and surprise, that there is not the least sign of any relaxation in my favour ; but I have hopes that, as I came to Venice solely with the object of recuperating my shattered health, the earnest representations of my physician may induce the Governor-General, his Imperial and Royal Highness Archduke Ferdinand Maximilian, to delay my expulsion till a warmer season of the year. However, in spite of these experiences, I now feel myself called upon to make one last effort to get my fate decided. I thought first of applying to the newly appointed Minister of Justice in Dresden ; only I fear all I should get from that quarter would be the usual unsatisfactory formal reply. Moreover, in thinking things over I became more conscious than ever how deplorably I had abused the position I once held in Dresden, and how hard it would be in consequence to find any influential person there to take up my badly damaged cause. Now I have reason to suppose that, however grievous may have been the differences—misunderstandings I would venture to call them —which arose between my honoured chief and myself, your Excellency has not altogether withdrawn that sympathy with my aims which was the cause of my Dresden appointment, and on which, in spite of all the trouble I gave you, I could always rely for protection and support. Furthermore, your kind and considerate behaviour to my wife encourages me to believe that such recollections as you have preserved of me are purged of any feeling of bitterness, so that I cannot help concluding that your Excellency is the one person appointed by Fate to be my final mediator at the Court of Dresden, and that I should be doing a great wrong were I to neglect the opportunity.

Therefore, in making this last and decisive appeal I would beg you, as my former friend and benefactor, to remember only the cordial relations that once existed between us ; to forgive me in a spirit of Christian charity for whatever wrongs I may have done you ; to blot out the past and see in me only a suffering mortal who needs protection and who craves your kind assistance.

So far as I can gather, his Majesty is resolved not to grant an amnesty to any of the refugees involved in the Dresden rising of 1849, except on the condition that the person concerned shall submit himself for trial and sentence, and this, I understand, is the only way in which

I could obtain my own pardon. I have therefore been seriously considering whether it would be advisable for me to adopt this course. On the one hand, I should suppose that no very heavy or serious charges could possibly be brought against me; indeed, when some of the chief points alleged were reported to me (in confidence) I at once saw them to be entirely unfounded, so that perhaps I could present myself for trial with some hope of complete acquittal.

If I had any compelling reason for such a course, if I wanted to return to my family, to take up a post, or to resume my position, which could only be done by a return to my own particular country, I should probably make the venture, even at the risk of a short imprisonment; but in my case no such consideration is involved.

After ten years of exile, entailing a complete loss of touch with my former sphere of artistic work, any return, even if offered to me, would no longer seem desirable. My health has long been precarious and liable to be impaired by overstrain, and this is now the case to a greater extent than before. I can no longer think of improving my circumstances by taking a permanent post with regular duties; it would soon kill me. All that makes me wish to return to Germany is the possibility of occasionally supervising the first productions of my operas at certain important theatres. Such a possibility, I own, if granted me, would have a beneficial effect on me, and give me a zest for future work. But even here my experience teaches me to be careful, and (having regard to the generally very inadequate abilities of German actors and singers) not to expect any particular pleasure or satisfaction from the rehearsals of my operas. Indeed, my sensitiveness with regard to the stage has, as I have verified by isolated experiences, become far keener during my ten years of complete seclusion in proportion as my ideals have grown loftier and more intellectual.

This temper of mind, which in part springs from the excessive sensitiveness of my nervous system, causes me seriously to consider whether I should not be recklessly endangering my health by exposing myself to the agitating

and tormenting chances of a trial, with a possible depriva-
tion of my liberty, a thing that could not fail to have an
injurious effect. I realize now, after ten years, during
which my views have completely changed, that I am not,
politically speaking, the same man. Those wild, unhappy days seem like the vague, confused images of a
dream, at which I can only shake my head in wonder.
And now, if I am to undergo a trial which may last for
months, and long, wearisome examinations on matters
that are mere shadows to me, but about which I shall have
to answer with the precision of a lawyer, if I am to be
confronted with any chance comer who fancies he once
observed something suspicious in my conduct, if I am to
live in dread of imprisonment for an act of folly long ago
repented, I can only conclude that this path to pardon is
closed to me by the nature of the case and its probable
effect on my health.

It is only by sparing myself, physically and mentally,
that I shall have strength to complete a whole series of
works, the germs of which are already in my mind,
and give them to the world as a possession. This consideration, together with a certain pride in my artistic
success, moves me definitely and finally, as I hereby declare
to your Excellency, to decline to take the way to pardon
that has been pointed out to me.

Under the circumstances I might well regret that, if I
was doomed to take my part in the follies of '49, I did
not do so as a subject of Baden, or Austria, or even Russia ;
for in that case I should have experienced the same leniency
which has long ago allowed those in like case with myself
to return to their countries by the annulment of the proceedings against them.

Though I must regard myself as shut off by this declaration from the only way at present open to me of returning
to Germany, I will not yet take it as final that I am irre-
vocably banished from my country (to which, by virtue
of my art, I belong as no other artist can) and condemned
to live and work in an alien environment, nor will I base
my future plans on this idea, until I receive your Excellency's definite answer, for which I earnestly entreat.

My consideration for my poor wife, so sorely tried, so great a sufferer, and her desire to find a settled home for life in her own German land, also urge me to make this request, which I regard as final and decisive.

I therefore humbly and earnestly beg your Excellency to take such steps as seem good to you, and to give me a definite answer on this point, whether, while absolutely rejecting the method of obtaining pardon which I have just discussed, I may hope for a speedy and merciful decision on the part of his Majesty as to my future fate or not.

I doubt if I should be able to find words for any fresh petition to the King, for I feel that in my letters to his Majesty and his Royal Highness Prince Albert I have already exhausted everything that I could adduce in my favour on this question. I can hardly venture to hope that even your Excellency's mediation will succeed in softening his Majesty's heart; but in case that should come about, I will touch on another matter in dispute between us, relating to my return to Germany and suggest how it might best be settled.

With regard to the loan of 5000 thalers made to me under royal guarantee from the Theatrical Pension Fund, I must suppose that, according to the usual practice in that department, this amount was put down to my account at the time, and probably in the statement concerning me presented to his Majesty by your Excellency; also that, considering my almost destitute position, there was no expectation of my being able to repay it; consequently, I have always felt that, in any case, I owed the deepest and most loyal gratitude to his Majesty, whose gift I must consider this sum to be, and I must try my best to give practical expression to my gratitude by any means in my power. To this effect, I would suggest to your Excellency the following agreement. I would bind myself for the rest of my life to offer every one of my works (of which I have several ready) free to the management of the Royal Court Theatre, and at any time, if they so desire, personally to conduct the rehearsals and first performances, and any others, of these works, for which purpose I should have to come to Dresden, but would require no payment ; in return for this undertaking all claims for the repayment of the former loan to be abandoned.

I confess that my wish to have this matter settled honourably is of considerable weight in impelling me to take this last step toward a possible return to Saxony. Furthermore, my present position in the artistic world justifies me in regarding my future participation in the musical life of Germany as a gain to my countrymen, as well as a satisfaction—though a limited one—to myself. Should this consideration fail to weigh in my favour, I must sorrowfully resign myself to my fate. In that case I must make up my mind once for all to work for foreign countries only. Though it will be hard and painful for me to overcome the difficulties of language where my dramatic works are concerned, I may perhaps find some support in a not altogether unjustified feeling of resentment. Enough for me that in such a case I should not need to make my own complaint of the harsh way in which I have been treated ; the silent letters on my tombstone would cry aloud to posterity.

But, whatever happens, I feel a weight off my mind now that I have explained my situation to my earliest benefactor, whom even now I hesitate to regard as wholly estranged. I leave it to your Excellency to choose the way that may seem best to you to make a final appeal for a definite decision of my fate, and I await your reply with the feeling that on it will depend whether I return to Germany or not. May God guide your heart and your actions ; of your wisdom I can have no doubt.

With deep respect and homage,
Your Excellency's obedient servant,
RICHARD WAGNER

CANAL' GRANDE, PALAZZO GIUSTINIANI
CAMPIELLO SQUILLINI, No. 3228

This letter reached von Lüttichau on February 14. Two days later he sent a distinctly cool reply, passing over the particular points raised in the letter and merely referring to the fundamental principle of the Saxon Government : [1]

> I have received your letter of the 9th on the 14th, and hasten to reply that it is not in my power to intervene on your behalf with any chance of success, seeing that no departure can be made from the established rule that an applicant for pardon must first present himself for trial and sentence, which you absolutely decline to do. It is still open to you to apply personally to his Majesty the King.
>
> v[on] L[üttichau]
>
> DRESDEN
> *February* 16, '59

We cannot now determine whether von Lüttichau made inquiries in the highest quarters as to the prospects of Wagner's appeal, and especially as to whether the new point—the idea of working off the old debt to the Saxon Theatrical Pension Fund by means of services rendered—should be taken into consideration. That von Lüttichau would refuse this last proposal on his own sole responsibility is exceedingly unlikely ; we may rather suppose that the King (who, as we can see by many other cases in the archives of the Ministry of Justice, reserved questions of pardon, especially the pardon of the May insurgents, to himself) gave, or caused to be given, the answer that the well-known principle was to be observed, and that pardon, or withdrawal of prosecution, could not be granted till sentence had been pronounced or trial undergone.

To a man with such a strict conception of legal right as King John possessed it was inconceivable that justice (that is, the proper punishment of a rebel) should be mixed up with a business deal, or, in other words, that an established right should be given up in order

WOLF ADOLF VON LÜTTICHAU, GENERAL MANAGER OF THE
DRESDEN COURT THEATRE
From a photograph.
Office of the Dresden State Theatre   110

to get a few operas cheap for the Court Theatre. Such a proposal might commend itself to some princely Mæcenas, but not to " the jurist among kings, the king among jurists," as Bluntschli called him in a lecture on German jurists.

In his letter Wagner mentions the steps taken by the Saxon Government to have him expelled from Venice. We must here go back a little. At the very beginning of Wagner's stay in Venice the Saxon Government was informed of the fact; the Austrian Government itself sent the news to Dresden. We have already seen how, in spite of much opposition, Wagner was allowed to spend a few months undisturbed—by politics, at least— in the City of the Lagoons. But early in 1859 this calm was broken; the Saxon envoy at Vienna had done his best to have the composer expelled. At the beginning of this year, just when Wagner, owing to Devrient's confident expectation that the intercession of the Grand Duke of Baden would be effective, was reckoning on entering Germany to produce *Tristan*, he had to ex- perience, once more, the implacable hostility of King John and his ministers.

Wagner states, in his autobiography, that the Saxon Ambassador—at that time Privy Councillor and Chamberlain Rudolf von Könneritz—had applied repeatedly at Vienna for Wagner's expulsion, as the friendly officials among the Venice police had often hinted to him. But these earlier requests from Saxony do not seem to have been couched in regular official form ; otherwise the Austrian Ministry could not have replied by asking whether Saxony was making a formal demand for Wagner's expulsion—in which case it was hinted that the demand might not be welcome, as Austria had to consider Switzerland, a friendly state, with regard to Wagner's passport. The matter went no further at the time. Whether things were actually as Wagner told Minna (January 16, 1859) on the strength of information received from a Ministerial *employé* at Vienna, it is hard to judge ; there is nothing about it in the correspondence of the Saxon Embassy at Vienna, nor in the correspondence between the Austrian authorities concerned, the Foreign Office and the Chief of Police at Vienna, and the Governor and the police authorities at Venice, which show no trace of any Saxon machinations, at least during the early months of his stay. There may have been a semi-official, but privately conveyed, suggestion made by the Ambassador, which could be disavowed in case of need, as there was no tangible proof of it.

The Chief of Police, General von Kempen, in his order of October 1, 1858, had provisionally allowed Wagner to stay at Venice, but wished that the Governor's office should instruct the police, as soon as Wagner's health improved, to induce him to quit Venice and the Austrian territory generally. In answer the Chief of Police at Venice, Franceschinis, on December 20 reported to the Governor as follows, substantially confirming the description in the earlier reports : [1]

VENICE
December 20, 1858

In consequence of von Bissingen's recommendation of October 8 and von Kempen's orders of September 9 :
Richard Wagner, the political refugee from Saxony, has been kept under close observation. He is lodged in the

Palazzo Giustiniani, No. 3228, by St Barnabas's, where his conduct, so far, has given us no cause for remark. He lives very much retired, and is employed solely with his musical compositions. In the work of transcription he is assisted by a certain Karl Ritter, whom he brought with him from Zürich. He plainly shows that he does not care to make any new acquaintances, which is explained by the fact that he suffers from nervous irritability. A month ago this was accompanied by an attack of erysipelas in one foot, which entirely prevents him from going out. In the next few weeks he will probably be able to leave the house for a stroll.

His correspondence is fairly extensive, but confined to the managers of the principal theatres—Weimar, Berlin, Zürich, Dresden, Darmstadt, and Leipzig—and the well-known composer Liszt. He is desirous of wintering here, in the hope of a complete restoration to health, and seems to have no intention of leaving Venice. In any case I will take great care that he does not go to any other part of the Empire without my knowledge.

FRANCESCHINIS
(*manu propriâ*)

Von Bissingen sent this report to Kempen at Vienna, with a covering letter of December 22, but no further comment. A month later followed a further report to von Bissingen from Crespi :

The well-known musical composer, Signor Richard Wagner, has quite recovered from the affection in his foot, which obliged him to keep his room, and can now be seen on fine days walking on the Riva degli Schiavoni.

He continues his retired mode of life, spending many hours a day in composing, and he does not seem to have received any visitors. A week ago Wagner sent his new opera *Tristan* to Baden, with a dedication to her Highness the Grand Duchess of that state, who not only deigned to accept the dedication, but was further pleased to express her gratification. It is said that his Highness the

Grand Duke also has sent him an autograph letter on the subject.

Signor Wagner has lately received an invitation from the Musical Society of Trieste, asking him to give some lectures on the new style of music, and it is known that he has declined the request on the ground that he did not consider himself authorized to move from here to another city of the Austrian monarchy, since the Austrian Ambassador at Berne had prescribed Venice alone as his place of residence.

Many lovers of music here—among them some distinguished foreigners like the Russian Prince Dolgoruki, himself a composer, and Princess Galitzin — have approached Signor Wagner on the subject of conducting a performance of some of his new compositions. As Wagner declared himself willing to do so without any prospect of payment, merely with a view to seeing the impression his new music would make, there was a plan formed for carrying out this idea with the orchestra of the Fenice, in the Apollinea Hall, but nothing definite has yet been settled.

Considering it my duty to bring all this to the knowledge of your Excellency, I take this opportunity to state my humble opinion as to the method in which we should proceed to carry out the order from headquarters, of December 22, 1858 (No. 6562.P), as to intimating to the aforesaid Signor Wagner that he should shortly leave the Imperial and Royal dominions. Having regard to the fame which he has won by his musical talents, we propose to summon him here and explain to him verbally the necessity of departure, reserving the formal notice for the event of his not complying with our warning.

The execution of the order will be carried out thus, unless your Excellency thinks fit to communicate orders to the contrary.

For the Imperial and Royal Chief of
Police, who is indisposed,
CHIEF COUNCILLOR CRESPI

On January 30, 1859, the Governor sent an abstract of this report, together with a letter from the Venetian police, to the Chief of Police at Vienna. Since Wagner "has now so far recovered that he can undertake a journey without any special danger to his health, he [von Bissingen] will ask the Deputy Chief of Police to give him a polite hint to leave Venice, and the Imperial territories generally." He would report the date of Wagner's departure when it occurred.

According to Wagner's account, it was owing to fresh pressure on the part of the Saxon Ambassador that the Austrian Government resolved to take a step which Count von Buol had formerly opposed; but at this time the attention of the Prime Minister was so completely engrossed by the threatening complications with Sardinia and France that the Chief of Police, an enemy of Wagner's, could do as he pleased; thus the order contemplated in von Bissingen's letter to Vienna soon followed. On February 3, 1859, as Wagner wrote to von Bülow, he was informed that he must leave Venice. Although the notice was given in a courteous manner, it was a heavy blow to him, as he wanted to get on with *Tristan*; in his indignation at the "monstrous spite of the Saxon Government," which he considered to blame, he was for leaving at once, "without trying to soften their cruel harshness." This is certainly an exaggerated way of putting it; the whole attitude of the Venetian police up till then had, on the contrary, been one of generous forbearance. The advice they now gave him for his future conduct was very useful to him; for it was they who counselled him to apply for a medical certificate in order to get permission for a longer stay from the highest authority in the Regno Lombardo-Veneto, the Governor-General, Archduke

Maximilian himself, the Emperor's brother. Wagner did so, and Max at once granted the required permission to stay longer, telegraphing to the local authorities not to trouble Wagner any more. The excitable and grateful Master was delighted when some time after, during a visit of the Archduke to Venice, he found a chance opportunity of mingling unknown in the crowds and greeting his protector.

The device which he had successfully employed in this case—not to defend himself or protest, but to put the whole matter on the score of his health, appealing to the consideration that a sufferer expects to receive from anyone not hostile to him—set him thinking, as he himself states (to Minna, on February 27), that he might try the same method in respect to Saxony.

In his letter to von Lüttichau of February 9, 1859, he had mentioned his state of health, but had declared that he would not adduce fresh reasons for his vindication or defence beyond what he had included in his petitions to the King himself and to the Crown Prince Albert. Now, however, the contrast between the failure of his long letter to von Lüttichau (given above) and the speedy success of his request " on grounds of health " to Archduke Max induced him to use his weak state as a reason for not surrendering for trial. He wrote a letter to the Minister of Justice which he had long been planning (since December 1858), and in which he had already thought of laying stress on the state of his health.

Ferdinand Zschinsky, the former Minister of Justice, had died on October 28, 1858. As one of the Ministers newly appointed by the King in

May 1849, he had been a zealous champion of royalty against revolution ; and King John, in grateful recognition of his services, raised him to the rank of an hereditary noble on May 3, 1856, and gave him a position of special influence as President of the Council of Ministers. Wagner believed (no doubt from information that reached him) that Zschinsky's place would not soon be filled up, and in a letter to Minna of November 14, he regarded this delay as a good sign, since it showed that people were wanting to see what would happen in Prussia about the amnesty, although, as a matter of fact, questions of administration were the only cause of the delay.

On November 4, 1858, Baron von Beust took over the Presidency of the Council, and von Behr, hitherto Minister of Finance,[1] who had been entrusted with the provisional administration of the department, became Minister of Justice. As the latter was not so closely connected politically with the counter-revolution, Wagner hoped that he would assume a less prejudiced attitude, and—to use his own expression in a letter to Minna of January 25, 1859—resolved to do his very utmost to make a friend of him.[2] He himself, on February 27, describes the statements about his ill-health as " rather exaggerated," and goes on, " The letter is so worded that if this does not induce them to forgo the condition [his personal surrender for trial, which he recognizes as in itself justified] nothing will ever persuade them to do so." The letter runs[3] :

RIGHT HONOURABLE SIR,
    Constrained by the necessities of my position, I venture to trouble you with a humble petition.

I may take it for granted that you know how my imprudent conduct during the political disturbances of 1849, and my apparent attitude during the lamentable events at Dresden in the May of that year, gave rise to charges against me, which I thought I might escape by flight. I need only mention, to explain my present position, that neither by the intercession of certain sovereign Princes nor by my own petition in writing, in which I confess my true repentance, have I been able to obtain his Majesty's pardon and permission for a free return to Germany. I have been given to understand, though only indirectly, that the main reason for my regrettable lack of success is the attitude adopted by his Majesty in all such cases hitherto, that the royal pardon can only be granted to those who have previously presented themselves for trial and sentence. I am very sorry that I did not appear before the court earlier—preferably just after those fatal events. I was then hindered by an *exalté* state of mind, which entirely disappeared many years ago, and my regret is all the greater since, so far as I understand the charges brought against me, I might well have expected to secure a lenient sentence, if not a complete acquittal.

But since then ten years have gone by, and I have so completely and entirely changed my political views that it would now be extremely hard and irksome for me to undergo examination as to matters and events that are now mere vague shadows to me, of whose details I have no clear recollection. As I have found by testing myself, it would be quite impossible for me to give any clear and consistent answer to most of the questions that would be put to me, so that on many points I could do no more than confess that I have no longer any definite recollection of the matter. But what makes me most apprehensive is my present state of health, which constitutes a serious danger for the future.

For a long time, and especially under the depressing influence of a ten years' exclusion from all possibility of a salutary distraction by the practical exercise of my art, my nervous system has developed such a degree of sensitiveness that it is only by the most careful following out of the prescriptions of my doctors that I have been able to keep my physical organs in any tolerable condition. Latterly, however, my sufferings have been so acute that a change of residence to the climate of Venice was necessary to effect an improvement in my condition, and enable me to continue my work.

It was this consideration that lately induced his Imperial and Royal Highness the Archduke, Governor-General of the Kingdom of Lombardy, to suspend the order for my expulsion (which, as I gather, was demanded by the Royal Saxon Government) on the ground of a medical certificate attesting my condition. As my return to Germany with a view to settling there permanently is desirable for many reasons, especially for the sake of my sorely tried wife, I have latterly consulted my physician as to whether I could, without serious danger to my health, expose myself to the excitements and shocks of an examination in court at my trial and to the inevitable longer or shorter term of imprisonment. He decidedly advised me not to think of such a step, if I did not want to shatter my health for ever ; my doctor knows me, and the nervous irritability that cripples all my physical functions, and is certain that I could not possibly run the risks of such a proceeding without absolute ruin to my health.

I therefore appeal to the kind and humane feeling of your Excellency, with the humble petition that you may consider my case sympathetically, and make a favourable report on it to his Majesty. I unreservedly acknowledge the justice of the conditions which his Majesty has laid down for granting a pardon. I confess my guilt with sincere repentance, as I did years ago, and acknowledge the justice of the attitude maintained toward me, nor would I seek to dispute it in principle. Yet I most humbly entreat his Majesty, through the mediation of your Excellency, mercifully to consider my impaired health, which would make it dangerous for me to submit to the conditions annexed to my amnesty, to waive these conditions on this sole ground, as in an exceptional case, and to allow me to share in the King's clemency without running a risk of incapacitating myself for further work, and thereby losing all the advantage of an amnesty.

I shall never cease to regard this gracious pardon as the greatest benefit I have ever received, and my whole life shall prove my gratitude. Moreover, I shall remain deeply indebted to your Excellency in particular for your kind advocacy and mediation.

With the expression of my highest respect and deepest submission, I remain,

Your Excellency's obedient servant,

RICHARD WAGNER

VENICE
CANAL' GRANDE, PALAZZO GIUSTINIANI
CAMPIELLO SQUILLINI, No. 3228
February 22, 1859

As Wagner himself expected, this letter was laid before the King. Von Behr wrote on the rough draft of his reply, " Wagner's letter, to which this is the answer, is to be sent to his Majesty. BEHR."

The answer, which was sent to Minna and which the Minister had drafted himself, must therefore be regarded as the King's own decision.

To the Wife of Kapellmeister Wagner

The rule that Saxon political refugees shall only be allowed to return on the condition that they submit to the trial which they evaded by flight has repeatedly been enforced and maintained. I am therefore not in a position to give your husband any hope that an exception will be made in his favour.

In accordance with your offer, I beg you will communicate the above to your husband, and so spare me the necessity of any further reply.

Yours obediently,

BEHR

Minister of State

DRESDEN
March 10, 1859

JOHANN HEINRICH VON BEHR, SAXON MINISTER OF JUSTICE
From a lithograph by O. Rafeld, inscribed, "Drawn from life by Mr Krantz.
Printed by L. Zöllner."
Municipal Museum, Dresden 120

Wagner must have received the answer, which his wife sent him at once, while still at Venice, though his letters to her contain nothing about its arrival. One more hope had thus come to nothing. People in Dresden were not so ready as they were in Milan to consider the reason, or pretext, of health as sufficient to warrant a remission of punishment. Implacability or, rather, a rigid adherence to the principle of legal right was so firmly established in the highest quarters that even a change at the Ministry of Justice was of no assistance.

Partly as a curiosity, and at the same time as a sign of a growing change of temper in certain loyalist circles at Dresden, we may mention the suggestion to which Wagner jokingly alludes in a letter to Minna (March 1, 1859). Minna, without having read it herself (at least so she says), had sent him a draft of a letter to the King that had been sent to her by a " man of high position." Wagner could only laugh at this well-meant but ill-written effusion, and took it for a joke of Minna's ; the King, he knew, was too astute to take such a letter seriously. Wagner sent the letter back to Minna on March 9.

On February 23, the very day after he had addressed his letter to Behr, Wagner wrote to Liszt suggesting the possibility of his petition being refused and declaring his readiness in that case to make one last attempt. He proposed to inform the Grand Duke of Baden of all the steps he had taken so far, and ask his permission to apply to the Emperor of Austria, the Prince of Prussia, the Grand Duke of Weimar, and the Duke of Saxe-Coburg-Gotha, begging them, either by direct agreement among themselves or by the aid of the Diet, to allow him to reside in their territories.[1]   To make this easier for the monarchs, he pointed out that such a step involved no hostility toward King John and that only his ill-health and nervous condition made it impossible for him to surrender for trial at Dresden, though he acknowledged this to be just, and would not suggest that the King should change his views— let the obligation of extradition be merely suspended, as an exception, in the interests of German art.   Whether this course should be followed must depend on the consent of the Grand Duke of Baden.   Wagner himself was not very sanguine about it, but in any case he wanted to have his position made clear.

The scheme was dropped, nor was any application made to the Grand Duke.   And, indeed, no more inauspicious moment could have been chosen ;   even art-loving princes had far more pressing anxieties for the future of Germany and the safety of their own states ;   they had to decide what action Prussia and the other states of the Confederation should take if France were to back up Sardinia in attacking Austria. This question, which was one of life and death for the Confederation, kept German statesmen busy for months.   Prussia's double position as a member of the Confederation and a Great Power made her attitude one of far-reaching importance, and Baden was the first state to be threatened in case of war between the German Confederation and France.   Only an artist without either political sense or knowledge of the world could have conceived the possibility of such a plan succeeding at such a time.

Wagner's stay in Venice, which was not intended to last longer than the cold season, now drew to an end, his departure being somewhat hastened by the political situation. On his way to Milan, on March 24, Wagner was held up by the massing of troops there, and after his safe arrival at Lucerne there was a long delay in the arrival of his baggage, which had been sent after him. The Austrian police did not fail to report his actual departure at Dresden through diplomatic channels, and the Dresden Foreign Minister then informed the Home Office and the Ministry of Justice of this re-assuring event.[1]

> Referring to its communication of September 24 of last year, the undersigned Ministry has the honour respectfully to inform the Ministry of Justice that the refugee Richard Wagner, as the Austrian Embassy here has just reported, in consequence of orders from the Chief of the Imperial Police, left Venice on the 25th of last month, and has gone to Lucerne.
>
> THE MINISTRY OF FOREIGN AFFAIRS
> BEUST
>
> DRESDEN
> *April* 13, 1859

Wagner stayed for five months at Lucerne, where his time was chiefly taken up with finishing *Tristan*, though he was also busied with plans for the future. As he could not stay there for ever, and did not wish to return to Zürich, by Liszt's advice he resolved, though with many misgivings and great reluctance, on moving to Paris, which he so disliked. In a letter full of bitter self-disparagement and complaints of himself, his friends, and the whole world, he wrote to Liszt on May 8, 1859:

123

It is frightfully unpatriotic to propose to make oneself comfortable in the very stronghold of the enemy of the German nation. Good Germans ought to do something to spare the most German of all German operatic composers this terrible trial. . . . Yet this, it seems, is what Germany will drive me to !

Liszt tried to quiet his hotheaded friend with a dose of strong common sense.

Minna, who was still unwilling to give up the idea of a Saxon amnesty, found her husband disinclined at first to go on with it. On April 24 he refused to waste another word on it ; on June 29 he declared that the answer he had received from the Minister of Justice was the end of everything. He rejected a fresh suggestion of Minna's on August 16 ; after the way he had been received hitherto he could not again write to the King of Saxony—it would be possible only if a guarantee of success was given, say through von Lüttichau. The difficulties raised as to getting a French visa for his new Swiss passport worried him for weeks. " Apparently they take me for a desperate conspirator, and certainly the way I have been treated by Germany gives some colour to the notion." He got his passport at last, on August 23.

But before he left Lucerne he had to send another refusal to Dresden. This time it was to Tichatschek, who had sung the part of Lohengrin with great success at the first performance in Dresden on August 6, and was at that time in correspondence with Wagner. Considering the latter's dislike for conducting, the expression in a letter of June 27, " Oh, God ! What would I give to be once more at the head of my orchestra ! " sounds strange. Also, on April 7 of that year he had written to Frau Julie Ritter that his ten years of exile had made him indifferent to being amnestied; it would give him no pleasure, he said, to work with von Lüttichau or even with Tichatschek. The latter proposed a fresh petition for pardon, which he would have presented to the King by an intermediary;[1] but Wagner was firm—he had nothing new to say to the King, and nothing to expect from him but contemptuous silence. Without an assured guarantee that a fresh petition would, so to speak, enable the King to change his mind, he would do nothing.

The curt way in which, in February, Lüttichau had dealt with Wagner's long and earnest letter, still rankled in his mind; and he was further annoyed because Lüttichau proposed simply to deduct the royalties on *Lohengrin* from Wagner's old debt to the Theatrical Fund, without even coming to an understanding as to the scale on which royalties were to be reckoned.

VI

WAGNER IN PARIS

1859–61

AFTER leaving Lucerne Wagner stayed a few days at Zürich, and reached Paris before the middle of September. At first he was still buoyed up by the prospect of eventually arranging a performance of *Tristan* at Karlsruhe; as late as October 5 he wrote hopefully to Otto Wesendonk, but by October 9 he told Minna that he was doubtful of the Karlsruhe plan, and was looking round for openings in other quarters. On the same day he wrote about the matter to Tichatschek; and by October 21 he had to tell Mathilde Wesendonk, " The idyllic dream of Karlsruhe has altogether vanished." This disappointment was the more grievous, since he had counted on some material benefit should *Tristan* prove a striking success. The failure of his plans made his position so difficult that, on January 1, 1860, he wrote to Mathilde that he was compelled to accept engagements as conductor in order to earn some money.[1]

Dresden too aroused fleeting hopes only to disappoint them. On October 27, 1859, he had written to Otto Wesendonk :

> The Manager at Dresden (Lüttichau) informs me (through Tichatschek) that he hopes to induce the King

of Saxony to have me recalled to Dresden for the first performance of *Tristan*, but this could not take place till next July. At any rate, I should get singers there with good voices. What shall I say to this?

And a week later, on November 4, 1859, he sent Tichatschek a long letter, mostly filled with complaints of Lüttichau's stinginess over *Lohengrin* :

> You know that originally I had not reckoned on getting any royalties in ready money from Dresden, and—well, I quite understand how much my position with regard to the Manager is changed by the fact that the advance made to me by the late King has been cancelled. But I wish Lüttichau would take the trouble to arrange for me to be recalled to Dresden to produce *Tristan* there ; if he can put this through I not only forgive his present stinginess, but will undertake never to demand or receive a penny for *Tristan* or any of my future works. If he cannot manage this, and if at some future time he wants to produce a new opera of mine without me, it will surprise him to see what he will have to pay for the score. It is scandalous how your people there treat us poor devils of composers. . . . And now one more serious word about the *Tristan* plan. If I could really be allowed to come—well, I don't mind even waiting half a year for the first performance.

On November 24 he again suggests to Tichatschek that the latter should ask Lüttichau in confidence whether he thinks " that he can get the King to give me a safe-conduct for four weeks ; if this were possible I would promise the first performance [of *Tristan*] for Dresden." But in December this plan also fell through.

On December 22, 1859, he complained bitterly in a letter to a musical editor that nobody was trying to get him amnestied, and this disloyal and cowardly attitude on the part of German artists compelled him to think of other outlets for his creative energy. But he wrote to Tichatschek on December 26, 1859, on hearing of Ignaz Lachner's supposed summons to Dresden, " Dresden seems to have quite done with me. Very well, then ! Good-bye ! " He never thought how often, during the last ten years, he had reviled and disowned not only his enemies and the Government at Dresden, but Dresden itself ; and now, when he was seeking to cast anchor in that undesired but necessary haven after all other moorings had broken, he was disgusted at the unfriendly temper of Dresden ! This seems rather too exacting, even to an impartial observer who by no means approves of the attitude of the Government.

The plan of giving concerts at Paris with selections from his works, and of having performances of his operas with first-class German singers (Tichatschek, Niemann, Bürde-Ney), was unsuccessful. The concerts, which occupied him most, took place on January 25 and February 1 and 8, 1860 ; their artistic success was great, but not sufficient to give him an assured position in the musical world of Paris. The financial results were even worse ; instead of a clear profit which would have helped him to carry out his plans for the future, there was a deficit, which added to his burden of debt. An attempt to repeat the Paris concerts at Brussels in the latter half of March was also a financial failure ; only two concerts were given, and the loss on these caused Wagner to cancel the third.

This sore disappointment, and the apparent hopelessness of getting leave to give a concert at the Grand Opéra, so dashed his hopes of Paris that he revived

JOSEPH ALOYS TICHATSCHEK
From a photograph.
Office of the Dresden State Theatre 128

the German plans, which he had practically abandoned, and resolved to make a fresh move in Dresden. In a letter to Liszt from Brussels (March 29) he says, " I am seriously thinking of settling my old differences with Dresden, if they will only make certain reasonable concessions." And in a letter to Mathilde Wesendonk on March 3 he had spoken even more plainly :

> I am seriously considering a new plan. Instead of undergoing all this drudgery and humiliation to make a success at Paris, why not take the risk of going to Dresden, being tried, sentenced, and, as I expect, amnestied ? Then I can have free access to the best theatre in all Germany, produce *Tristan* there, and break the spell that now binds me. . . . It seems unpardonably selfish for me to spare myself any trouble or disgrace that might lead to the production of my work.

When he wrote thus his failure at Brussels had not yet occurred ; but when this hoped-for source of profit dried up, and his income was at a lower ebb than ever, he had to snatch at a fresh chance of returning to Saxony. This time he hit on another way of approach ; he applied to the Saxon Ambassador, with whom he had become slightly acquainted two years before. As he wanted to protect his copyright in the piano editions of his works and the rights of representation of his operas in France, he needed the help of the official Saxon representative at Paris. He wrote on January 21, 1858, to Minna that this affair would bring him into touch with the Saxon Ambassador, which would be very amusing. Whether he was allowed to indulge in the " amusement " of worrying the Ambassador himself or whether this merely formal business was done in the chancery of the Embassy is not known.

The Saxon Ambassador was Baron Albin Leo von Seebach,[1] a man who took an intelligent interest in art. Wagner now applied to him, and had a kindly reception. Von Seebach's friendly attitude may have been partly due to the fact that Wagner had meanwhile found friends in high places at Paris; through Hans von Bülow he had been introduced to the Prussian Ambassador, Count Pourtalès, and his *attaché*, Count Hatzfeld, and Pourtalès' friendly help was useful to him during the whole time he spent at Paris. Hatzfeld had introduced him again to Frau Maria von Kalergis (*née* Countess Nesselrode), whom he had met before.

Through Princess Pauline Metternich, the wife of the Austrian Ambassador, the Emperor Napoleon III himself became interested in Wagner, and swept away all the opposition of his enemies by giving a direct command to produce *Tannhäuser* at the Grand Opéra.

It is plain that von Seebach, as Saxon Ambassador, could hardly adopt a haughty or hostile attitude toward one who, besides being patronized by the diplomatic representatives of the two chief German Powers, was also clearly in high favour at the Tuileries. Moreover, we get the impression that the Ambassador, quite apart from any question of Court or Society, was moved to espouse the cause of the composer by his personal liking for the man. As Wagner himself states, von Seebach " showed his sincere sympathy," [2] a feeling which may well have been strengthened by the fact that Frau von Kalergis was the cousin of von Seebach's wife (also a Countess Nesselrode), to whom Liszt himself applied some time afterward, in order to get into touch with the Ambassador.

On May 10, 1860, Wagner mentions, in a letter from Paris to Härtel, that the Saxon Ambassador there would soon be in Dresden personally, to remove the present difficulties in the way of the composer's re-admission into Germany. Just about this time the decisive step was taken: Wagner called on von Seebach, and in an exhaustive interview found occasion to give the Ambassador all possible assurances of his regret for the past and the absolute blamelessness of his present attitude ; he also stated his wishes for the future. We are well acquainted with the nature of this interview through a letter, written on May 16 by Wagner to von Seebach himself, which we must there-fore regard as trustworthy in its statements.

Honourable Sir,

In accordance with your Excellency's kind permission, I venture in the present letter to seek your valuable re-commendation and mediation, in order to effect a change in my political position as regards his Majesty the King, our august monarch.

In the course of the interview which your Excellency kindly granted me I gathered from your sympathetic expressions that you were reassured by what you heard from me, and were satisfied with my explanations. I acknowledged with perfect frankness the excitement of feeling that had made me, in a time of trouble, lose sight of many salutary and necessary considerations, and caused me, by my inconsiderate conduct, to draw down on my-self serious suspicions of criminal actions—a charge from which I unfortunately neglected to clear myself at the right time.

But with even greater confidence I can assure your Excellency that I am not conscious of having committed any really criminal act; still less do I remember having been concerned in any action of any sort by which I consciously assumed an attitude of hostility to his Majesty the late King, an act which would have been a mark of the blackest ingratitude toward a benefactor whom I shall never forget and shall always honour. I may further hope that by my frank explanations I completely satisfied your Excellency that that state of excitement (entirely alien from my real character) which carried me away under the pressure of unwonted circumstances and misunderstandings has entirely vanished, and that if it was ever possible for me to join a revolutionary political faction (with whom I really had nothing in common), my present views, the result of ripe experience, and my consequent future conduct, cannot possibly bring me into even apparently criminal relations with such a body. Your Excellency declared yourself convinced that as it was my frank and full return to art which cured me of that unfortunate madness, so it is only the interests of art that now actuate me, and that if I now long so ardently to be free to return to my native land my sole object is the practice of my art. I was very glad to find your Excellency admit that my whole artistic individuality is bound up with my German fatherland; and, in fact, the present is just the moment when no one could well doubt my sincerity in advancing this plea—now, when I have the prospect of a fine production of one of my music-dramas at the first theatre in France, and can yet declare that my highest ambition is to return to Germany in order to have my new works first performed, as they ought to be, in German, and before a German audience.

Your Excellency was assured, lastly, that in order to earn the privilege of a free return to Germany, I am quite ready to submit myself to a legal trial on the charges brought against me. I am induced to promise this by my conviction that no real offence could be proved against me, since I am not conscious of having committed any. But though I may think it a wise step to take this direct way to justify and absolve myself, yet, on the other hand, human weakness causes in me an unconquerable reluctance to submit myself for trial after eleven long years. That unhappy time seems to me like a dark and distant shadow ; when I think of it my recollections are confused, and it seems impossible to give clear and definite answers to the questions written down so long ago. If your Excellency will take into consideration the anxieties of a longer or shorter imprisonment, which in my present susceptible state of health might well have serious consequences, I believe I may count on your sympathetic consideration when I ask you again, and most earnestly, for your kind intercession to obtain a more lenient procedure in my case.

Hence I venture earnestly to beseech you, as my honoured patron, to recommend me to the favour of his Majesty in any way that may seem good to your Excellency. I am convinced that I have given you all the information necessary to enlighten our august monarch as to my case, and, emboldened by your kind assurance, I have every confidence (as far as one can be sure of anything human) that your Excellency will succeed in winning his Majesty's gracious pardon for a man who has erred, but has been sufficiently punished for his folly, and henceforth has no other desire than to do honour to his country by the practice of his art.

Will your Excellency rest assured of my deepest and sincerest gratitude, which I shall always cherish for my illustrious patron, and permit me, with the expression of my unbounded esteem and homage, to remain

Your Excellency's obedient servant,

RICHARD WAGNER

16 RUE NEWTON,
  CHAMPS-ÉLYSÉES
    PARIS
  May 16, 1860

Apparently Wagner's application to von Seebach was, if not caused, at least hastened by the latter's approaching journey home ; for on May 21, 1860, Wagner writes to von Bülow that he can settle nothing about moving to other quarters " till Herr Seebach is back from Dresden, where he hopes to get me amnestied by the King.   Seebach is a very good fellow, and has given me sound advice." To the same effect is his letter of June 5, 1860, to Otto Wesendonk :

> The Saxon Ambassador here, a very good fellow, is at present at Dresden, and will try to settle my affair personally with the King. Even now I can scarcely hope for success ; but if it were to come, and Germany were once more open to me, I hardly know of any theatre that possesses all the resources necessary for producing my work.

Berlin had practically nothing, Vienna was decadent.

> Dresden itself, which possesses the most suitable artists, would still remain closed against my personal presence and co-operation, which are so indispensable.

He expressed his hope of an amnesty next day in a letter to Härtel, and also in a conversation with Louis Schlösser, afterward Court Kapellmeister at Darmstadt, who met him in Paris on June 19. " My exile, I hope," said Wagner, " will not last much longer, if only we can convince the authorities that I am not dangerous. . . . Judge for yourself how far my fight against the false position of opera in this country resembles a political conspiracy."

Von Seebach worked zealously at Dresden to win for Wagner the wish of his heart, but at first met with little response from his chief, von Beust, the Foreign Minister and President of the Council, who had to ascertain and represent the personal views of King John. The chief ground for this opposition lay in the suspicion with which the King regarded Wagner's assurances that he had no longer any connexion with revolutionists and other dangerous people. Police

ALBIN LEO, BARON VON SEEBACH, SAXON AMBASSADOR
AT PARIS
From an oil-painting of 1847 in the possession of His Excellency Count Nikolaus
von Seebach.

134

spies had for years been industriously reporting on all suspicious persons who associated with Wagner or happened to cross his path ; note was taken of his casual or more intimate relations, his personal intercourse or correspondence with Herwegh, Semper, Heine (the Dresden scene-painter), Kietz, Malvida von Meysenbug, Kinkel, Rémenyi, and others.[1] All this, together with his polemical writings during his first year at Zürich and many stray utterances, which may not always have been discreet, had created and kept alive an impression that so restless a spirit was capable of any revolutionary act. We can see how suspicious of him people were, and not in Saxony only, by the difficulty that the French Ambassador in Switzerland made in giving Wagner a visa for his journey to France—even in August 1859 this mere formality was made dependent on the result of inquiries in Paris.

For some years Wagner had spoken of his complete withdrawal, not only from revolutionary opinions, but from politics generally. When he wished to settle in Paris in 1859 he published in the papers a protest against the idea that he was " a musical Marat." " My compositions have no revolutionary tendencies, as people are fond of saying. Even the King who has banished me allows my operas to be performed in his capital, and applauds them."

Meanwhile Wagner found an advocate in another quarter; Princess Augusta of Prussia had long been friendly toward him, and she was now informed by Pourtalès of Wagner's difficult position.

The favour shown to the German composer at Paris

by Napoleon's command may have awakened among Germans of high rank who were not really hostile a feeling that something ought to be done for him;[1] in any case, the presence of the Kings of Bavaria, Würtemberg, Saxony, and Hanover at Baden-Baden in the middle of June 1860, on the occasion of the meeting between King William of Prussia and Napoleon III, gave Princess Augusta an opportunity of speaking to King John about Wagner and putting in a good word for him.[2] When von Seebach first raised the question at Dresden his assurances that Wagner had finally and absolutely broken with revolutionary circles had not caused much change in the attitude of the Government, for his letter to von Beust of July 1 (see below) gives us to understand that he was not yet in a position to make any definite promise to Wagner; but in a personal interview he gave him some hope that people in Dresden were not altogether averse from showing leniency, in case he (Seebach) could adduce definite grounds for such a course in the shape of fresh declarations from Wagner himself. In his sympathy for Wagner he was all the more zealous to do something for him, but the matter was not so easy as Wagner supposed.

As soon as von Seebach returned to his post at Paris Wagner called on him, and was frankly informed of the attitude and views of the Dresden Government.

Immediately after this conversation Wagner sat down and wrote the following letter to the Ambassador.

PARIS
June 30, 1860

MY LORD BARON,

In spite of the high hopes aroused by the information which I received from your Excellency in the interview you most kindly gave me yesterday, I fear I must conclude that reports have lately been circulated concerning me in the highest quarters at Dresden—reports which, if they contained any truth, would make me appear quite unworthy of any favour from his Majesty the King. In the face of accusations such as these, that I was constantly in treasonable converse with members of some political party or other, I should be helpless if I could not declare with absolute frankness in the most positive manner that these reports, from what source soever they arise, are utterly false and slanderous.

As my life has been for a good many years a retired one, practically confining me to my house, and devoted exclusively to the labours of my art (so that no outside observer could possibly have caught me in any suspicious surroundings), my surprise that it should be possible to circulate such a damaging report about me is somewhat lessened by the obvious explanation that it is an absolute invention. Its origin is hard to determine.

Let me assure your Excellency that it is distasteful and painful to me to find that, owing to a mistaken judgment of my former conduct—with no justification except my apparent political position for so long—I am open to the reproach of belonging to some political party, regarded by its adherents as one of themselves and by others as one of their accomplices. Though I have never frequented public places or public meetings of any sort, the similarity of our position abroad brought me into touch with certain members of that party in the earlier years of my exile ; but any nearer acquaintance could only tend to undeceive them as to my attitude, so that I was always surprised at still having to contradict the false impressions prevailing as to my views. However, it is now many years since I have had occasion to do this, so that, not having had even the most innocent relations with those who are in the same position as myself, I can only refer the reports current about me to a personal spite, excited by annoyance at my real attitude.

If now your Excellency, fully accepting my assurances, will undertake to guarantee my honesty I pledge you my

137

word of honour that any report which represents me as having any criminal, or even suspicious, relations with any political party is absolutely baseless, and I cannot reproach myself with the slightest lapse in this respect, even in a moment of weakness. On the contrary, I am ready to expose as false any misuse of my name in this connexion. I also pledge my word of honour that, in case his Majesty the King graciously allows me to return to Germany, I will take the greatest care never at any time or in any place to give cause for a misunderstanding of my present political attitude by taking part in any demonstrations which could arise only from such misunderstanding. I promise to do my best to avoid such demonstrations, since I, as an artist, should be the chief sufferer from them. I authorize your Excellency to make any use you please of my declarations as soon as you hear of the slightest rumour that would throw doubt on my good faith.

I hope, however, that when I return to Germany I shall be able to show the world that a man who could compose such extensive and elaborate works as I have to show has spent the time of his exile in something else than senseless political agitation. On that point there will soon be no possible doubt ; and that is my chief reason for longing to be restored to the one and only country where those works can be given to the world.

Will your Excellency forgive me for troubling you with this letter ? Although your kind personal assurances might seem to render it unnecessary, I could not help writing, since I felt I ought to give a definite and frank declaration to my good friends and advocates, who, I am sure, will now be satisfied.

Will your Excellency accept the assurance of my most sincere and heartfelt thanks, and of the unbounded esteem and respect with which I have the honour to remain

Your Excellency's obedient, humble servant,

RICHARD WAGNER

16 RUE NEWTON,
CHAMPS-ÉLYSÉES

There is a slight discrepancy in the dates. Wagner speaks in his letter, which was dated June 30, of the interview of "yesterday," which was thus on the 29th, while von Seebach in his letter of July 1 also speaks of "yesterday," which would be on the 30th. Probably the first conversation took place on the 29th, and the written declaration was handed in on June 30. In any case, the difference is of no importance; it is certain that June 30 was the decisive day on which Wagner handed in a written declaration of the most precise and definite kind, to which he pledged his word of honour. This assurance not only entirely convinced von Seebach, but gave him an opportunity for approaching his royal master and his Ministerial chief on behalf of the exile. His sympathy was the keener since a well-intentioned subscription among diplomatic circles to cover the deficit on Wagner's concerts had, as von Seebach heard, proved a failure.

When, therefore, Wagner, immediately after drawing up the document we have just given and only a few hours after his interview, sent the letter to the Ambassador on June 30, the latter had no hesitation in forthwith sending a report of its contents, and especially of the purport of the conversation, to Dresden. In this report—without departing from his own strong Conservative views—he warmly pleaded Wagner's cause. It was a step that did von Seebach honour; for he, though a Saxon noble and an official belonging to the Court circle, proved his freedom from prejudice and the courage of his convictions by stating his views in the face of King John's well-known hostility and the unfriendly, or at best indifferent, attitude of von Beust. Seebach did so in the following autograph letter to the President of the

Council and Minister for Foreign Affairs, Baron von Beust :

PARIS
July 1, 1860

MY DEAR FRIEND AND CHIEF,

Richard Wagner came to see me yesterday, to hear what ground he has for hopes and fears. As I knew that during my absence his position had become more difficult (for the subscription to cover the debts incurred by his concerts here completely failed), I could not bring myself to deny him all hope of his Majesty's pardon.

I have in no way anticipated his Majesty's decision, but have only taken this opportunity of making it clear how far I have made myself responsible for the truth of his assurance that he heartily repents of his past errors, and for many years has kept purposely out of all political intrigues.

In the course of a very searching discussion of his present way of life I did not conceal from him that serious and apparently well-founded suspicion had been excited by reports that had lately come in concerning him [1]—of course, I did not mention from what sources. In answer Wagner swore with tears in his eyes that he knew of nothing that could have given the slightest reason for the charge of his being still connected with the party of 1848. After long reflection he could remember only that he had, six months ago, asked the painter Zychlinsky,[2] who was now as completely cured of seditious views as Wagner himself, to his house. He absolutely denied that he had had any other intercourse with any of the refugees of that time.

A few hours after our conversation Wagner sent me the enclosed letter, in the hope that his positive declaration that he had openly broken off his former connexions might make a favourable impression on his Majesty the King.

In now submitting the decision on this question to your consideration, dear friend and chief, I have only one argument to add to the reasons you know already which have made me, though a strong Conservative, an advocate for Wagner—the assurance that after our last conversation I could not possibly entertain any doubt as to his views.

With all due respect,

Yours obediently,

Von Seebach

Seebach's honest advocacy met with success. Many outside considerations helped him. The numerous prisoners of the May revolt who had suffered under the rod of Governor Heink (literally, according to Röckel's account) in the Waldheim Prison had been released—the last civilians in the autumn of 1859, the last soldiers in the spring of 1860 [1]—so that the stiff-necked republican Röckel, who would not consent to petition for pardon, was the only one not amnestied.

Thus there was really no good reason for withholding the amnesty any longer from Wagner, who had been so prodigal of pleas for pardon and assurances of penitence, especially as the granting of this favour would also gratify a German princess, as well as several Princes of the Confederation.

Von Beust received von Seebach's letter on July 10, 1860, and took the earliest opportunity of submitting it to the King, with Wagner's statement annexed. King John gave way, as far as he thought himself obliged, but without receding from the legal stand-point he had taken from the first. He would not have a man whom he evidently disliked back in Saxony ; but if other German princes and states liked to admit him for artistic reasons—well, they might. Von Beust himself drafted the answer to the Ambassador at Paris. The minute, in his own handwriting, is still extant, and is of especial interest on account of the alteration made in the original text before it was dispatched. Von Beust laid his minute before the King for his approval; and we can see how rigorously King John insisted on making his own attitude perfectly clear—he would concede to the composer nothing more than he could help. While in von Beust's original draft Wagner was to be allowed to apply in person to the Saxon Government if he required to go to any place within the German Confederation, King John preferred not to have any direct dealings with him; the permission from the Saxon authorities had to be applied for at Dresden through the Government of the state to which Wagner intended to travel. With this alteration the dispatch was forwarded to Paris on the same day.

DRESDEN
July 15, 1860

To THE KING'S AMBASSADOR,
BARON VON SEEBACH, PARIS

I have not failed to lay your Excellency's private letter of the 1st inst., with the enclosure, before his Majesty, and am able, in accordance with his august decision, to state as follows :

As I have repeatedly given your Excellency to understand, his Majesty, in dealing with petitions for pardon from those concerned in the revolt of 1849, holds fast to the principle that such persons as have escaped trial by flight should first present themselves for trial in person before their petition can be considered. I have also had to remind your Excellency that the personal circumstances in the case of the former Kapellmeister Richard Wagner are not such as would justify making an exception in his favour.

His Majesty, therefore, is still disinclined to grant a

pardon to Wagner,[1] who, if he should enter this country, would be immediately arrested.

However, his Majesty has no wish to prevent Wagner from entering other states of the Confederation, in order personally to conduct the performance of his compositions;[2] should he have occasion to do so, and should the Government of the state concerned request that no demand be made for his extradition, his Majesty is ready to accede to such a request. Of course, this concession is revocable, and will be withdrawn if Wagner gives cause by his conduct. Will your Excellency inform him of the foregoing?

BEUST

Seebach received the letter on July 20, and did not fail to inform Wagner in writing on the 22nd of the King's decision. Though it was not a full amnesty, still it was something, and might pave the way to complete rehabilitation. Wagner was therefore glad of it at first, and conquered his pride so far as to address to King John on July 26 the letter of thanks given below, which he sent to the Ambassador, with a request to forward it.

Von Seebach complied with his wish and dispatched it on July 29, with a few words of formal introduction to the Saxon Ministry of Foreign Affairs. Wagner's letter reached Dresden on August 1, and must have been submitted to the King at once, since on August 5 the original was returned to the Ministry to be filed for reference.

MOST SERENE MONARCH,
    AUGUST KING AND LORD,
    I have to thank your Majesty's gracious clemency that allows me (as I gather from a communication from your Majesty's Ambassador at Paris) freely to enter any

143

state of the German Confederation where I am called for the purpose of giving performances of my musical works, provided that I observe the necessary conditions.

This concession provides for all that is most important for the development of my artistic productions, and in return for this great favour I feel compelled to the present expression of my deepest and most sincere gratitude, which I herewith lay at the foot of your Majesty's throne, with the respectful request that you will graciously receive it.

Will your Majesty allow me to add to this expression of my sincere gratitude the assurance that, if I make use of your Majesty's gracious permission for the promotion of my artistic interests, I shall always and everywhere so conduct myself that your Majesty will have no cause for dissatisfaction with me and will not feel that I am unworthy of his goodness?

With the deepest respect and most entire submission, I remain,

Your Majesty's obedient subject,

RICHARD WAGNER

PARIS
July 26, 1860

Although it may have been hard enough for Wagner to squeeze out suitable expressions of respectful thanks, still, he had some cause for satisfaction; but his temperament hardly ever allowed him the undisturbed enjoyment of any good fortune, any success, or the attainment of any aim. So his feeling of relief in this case was blent with the weary disgust caused by long years of vain struggle. On that very 22nd of July, still under the impression caused by his partial amnesty, of which he had just heard, he writes to Mathilde Wesendonk:

So I can assure you, with a strange feeling of satisfaction, that the news I had a few days ago [1] of the withdrawal of the ban against entering Germany left me quite cool and unmoved. People sent me telegrams of joyful congratulation ; I have not answered any of them. Who would understand me if I told him that this only opens out to me a fresh field for suffering, a suffering so far outweighing any possible satisfaction that I may derive from it that I can only see a prospect of fresh sacrifices ?

A man like Wagner, impulsive and passing from one extreme of feeling to its opposite almost without transition, could not follow Horace's advice,

Æquam memento rebus in arduis
Servare mentem ;

not for him the fine, serene equanimity of his friend Liszt, or the cool self-restraint of a man of the world. The prospect of producing his operas in Germany called up before his eyes a vision of long, nerve-racking toil in dealing with the rancour of personal rivalries and the weariness of rehearsals. Whenever during his years of exile he conducted a rehearsal himself his bitterness of spirit over this thankless task always broke out afresh ; and now he was dreading an endless series of such exhausting struggles.

But his state of mind soon became more cheerful ; a trip to the Rhine promised a short respite from the strain of his work at Paris. In July he had sent Minna to Soden in the Taunus to take the cure ; he now planned to fetch her away, to pay a visit of thanks to Princess Augusta of Prussia, and then take a trip up the Rhine. Von Seebach had strongly advised him to give this expression to his gratitude, and had hinted that such a step would also please the King of Saxony, and Pourtalès gave him an introduction to the Princess's lady-in-waiting. He therefore resolved to extend his journey to Baden-Baden, where Augusta had gone.

In the autobiography he wrote later Wagner expressed himself rather coldly, almost negatively, about this interview, which took place in the pump-room. This tone may be due to the fact that the hopes of further assistance which he had based upon Augusta's patronage were unfulfilled, for he had openly expressed his intention, "without making any request, to satisfy myself whether I could expect any help from the lady in producing my new works." The accounts that he wrote immediately afterward to Liszt and Otto Wesendonk are not so unfavourable.

But the sight of the Fatherland left him quite unmoved, as he very plainly states. "Alas! I did not feel the slightest thrill at treading once more on German soil. Heaven knows I was absolutely cold!" His visit was too short, and he was not in the right humour to enjoy the beauties of the Rhine country, especially as his hoped-for visit to Liszt proved impossible. After six days he hurried back to work at Paris.

He realized fully that he was only partially amnestied. He writes to Liszt on September 13 :

My position with regard to Germany is still very difficult. You know that I have been neither amnestied nor pardoned ; they have only promised that no demand will be made for my extradition in case I want to enter a German state in order to produce my works, and its Government gives its consent and applies for permission to the Saxon Government. I could not even have extended my six days' trip to the Rhine as far as Weimar, without first fulfilling these conditions, unless I wanted to offend the Saxon Government at the very start. Our German princes, too, can never deal with me direct, as I am still under the ban. I cannot therefore hope for any important action in my favour from any Court, and the plans for producing my latest works are not much advanced.

He has great hopes of *Tannhäuser* at Paris, thanks to the high patronage of the Emperor, and wishes he could have the same help from a German prince.

I feel terrified when I think of Germany, and my future enterprises there. God forgive me ! I can see nothing there but miserable pettiness, a mere show and boast of sterling worth, without any real foundation, everything and everybody half finished. I must confess that my return to German soil did not make the slightest impression on me. Believe me, we have no real country ! And if I am a German, I carry my Germany in my heart.

Such passionate outbursts are not to be taken too seriously, for, in spite of his irritable and sarcastic temper, Wagner was too true a German to turn away from his country for long. " Cling to thy fatherland, thine own dear land. . . . Here are the mighty sources of thy strength." If these words spoken at Attinghausen applied to any German artist they were true of Wagner ; he himself felt this clearly, and has expressed it in his writings. He was soon enough to learn the bitter lesson that not even the Imperial favour, and the support of his enthusiastic friends, could give him and his art a real home by the Seine. Now and then the conviction that he expressed to Mathilde Wesendonk on March 3, " I don't believe in a French *Tannhäuser* or a French *Lohengrin*, still less in a French *Tristan*," was pushed out of sight by the apparent enthusiasm of the *Tannhäuser* rehearsals ; but too soon, and too cruelly, he was to realize that

> There in an alien world thou stand'st alone,
> A swaying reed that every storm may break.

Autumn and winter went by in Paris in a constant struggle with opposing forces, and illness hampered Wagner for some time in his work, but early in 1861 he cast all obstacles aside and reached his goal. On March 13, 1861, the first performance took place at the Grand Opéra, and, in spite of all opposition, developed into a success ; but the second performance, on March 18, ended in catastrophe. All Wagner's energy, all the loyalty of the artists, the support of the Corps Diplomatique, even the patronage of Napoleon and Eugénie, failed before the contemptible intrigues of an aristocratic clique of the Jockey Club, a frivolous set of men-about-town and protectors of the *corps de ballet*. They drowned the applause of the enthusiastic audience, and the energetic protests of Wagner's friends, by a horrible noise of whistles and all sorts of rowdy instruments. One of his most active champions was von Seebach, who, as Wagner testifies, tried so hard to shout down the fashionable mob that he was completely voiceless next day.

After the third attempt, which also was a scene of disorder, Wagner abandoned all future performances ; the warm appreciation of his kind French friends and the sincere sympathy of his German helpers and patrons were not enough to make up for his great sacrifice of time and labour, and for the loss of the reward he had expected—of which, in his perpetual financial embarrassments, he stood in bitter need. It was only through the generous and kindly assistance of his old friends, the Metternich and Pourtalès families and others, that Wagner was rescued from absolute want.

In April and May he visited Karlsruhe and Vienna, and the enthusiastic reception of *Lohengrin*, which he heard for the first time on the stage at Vienna on May 15, was balm for the wound that Paris had dealt him. However, in the summer he had to return to Paris, to break up his establishment there. Minna went to Soden for the cure, and Wagner himself stayed in the hospitable house of Pourtalès, which was a real haven of refuge for him. But he realized that he could not rest content with his present permission to stay in Germany, hedged about as it was with restrictions and conditions, and he felt it necessary not to lose sight of a complete amnesty. He at once applied to von Seebach, as is shown by the postscript to his letter to Minna of July 16, 1861, " Seebach hopes soon to get me amnestied in Saxony." But matters were not to go so speedily, and many disappointments had first to be endured.

VII

FINAL SUCCESS

1861–62

Further Steps taken by von Seebach and Minna at Dresden—
Wagner's Fresh Petition to King John—Full Amnesty.

WITH the end of July the Paris period of Wagner's life, which had lasted nearly two years, came to a close. He went *via* Soden to Weimar,[1] where he met with fresh disappointments. The Grand Duke, before March 1861, had intended to bestow on Wagner the Cross of the First Class of the Weimar Order of the Falcon, and had communicated his intention in a most gracious letter to his Minister, von Watzdorf. But the latter, who was no friend to Wagner, succeeded in checking Charles Alexander's friendly impulse, and an appeal from Liszt, to which the Grand Duke was ready to listen, was also unsuccessful, because people at Dresden, when inquiries were made from Weimar, had declared that in such a case the Knights of the Order in that city would send back their decorations. What a contrast do we find in the attitude of really noble natures, like those of his Paris friends Metternich, Pourtalès, and von Seebach, and their wives, who acted as true friends to the composer in his need! The Grand Duke dared not expose himself to such an insult, if any member of Dresden Court society would really have ventured on such an incredible piece of rudeness as sending back his decorations; so the

White Falcon of Weimar never perched on Wagner's breast. Though the Master was not much affected by this loss when Liszt told him of it,[1] still he felt bitterly this fresh proof that Saxon influence was a perpetual stumbling-block in his way. He writes about it to Minna :

> There will be no change here till I get a full amnesty from Saxony. So I shall wait to see what Seebach can manage to do ; but with the present wretched state of feeling at Dresden I can cherish very little hope, and must accustom myself when forming plans for the future not to reckon on any help from German princes, though I am glad to have got even so far as to be able to stay unmolested in Germany. However, this last experience has had one result : of course I quite withdraw my suggestion that you should settle in Dresden.

He does not forbid her to choose Weimar as a residence, but has a decided preference for Karlsruhe, where she could live modestly but comfortably and give him the possibility of again having a home of his own.[2]

In August Wagner left Weimar for Vienna, but his stay here, owing to the endless delays in putting on *Tristan*, was not good for his temper. Still, he hoped for good results in some respects, as he tells Minna on August 26. " Though I am in ill odour at Dresden, I think that in a few months (after I have been properly spied on and reported on at Vienna) my fortune there will undergo a complete change." However, this hope, like so many others, soon vanished. On October 16 he writes :

> You must not blame me if I look on the dark side of things, and ask myself what will come of it all, and whether I shall really have to die before people realize what they ought to have done to keep such a man alive.

Still, he does not lose faith in von Seebach's help. " I wrote to Seebach lately ; it is important that we should settle the Dresden business as soon as possible." And three days after he repeats that he has just written to von Seebach that the amnesty is of the greatest importance.

When Minna went to Dresden and wanted to settle there for good he agreed to her proposal, and reverted to the old Dresden plan of a house with a room for himself. But the idea of the amnesty was always in his mind. " If you can help to make it possible for me to stay a while in Dresden, do your best! You will find the way paved for you : I rely on Seebach's kindness for that."

Affairs in Dresden seemed to be developing favourably and to warrant higher hopes. Minna was well received everywhere, not only by her old friends and acquaintances and her former physician, Pusinelli, who attended her again, but by the General Manager von Lüttichau, who placed a seat in the theatre at her disposal. Wagner was moved to write and thank him, with the request that he would reserve the seat for her during her stay. It was evident that a cautious and correct Court official like von Lüttichau— though he could do pretty much as he liked in his distribution of free seats—could not in this case have given proof of his friendly feeling to the wife of a proscribed rebel of evil reputation, still admittedly disliked by the King, if he had not made discreet inquiries in the highest quarters.

At the end of November Wagner left Vienna. He travelled *via* Mainz back to Paris, full of a new idea for a brighter, more popular piece, which would help him over the weary time of waiting for the production of *Tristan*. This was *Die Meistersinger*. But even this joyous and stimulating task, and his hopes of being able to spend the summer months of the next year quietly on the Rhine, could not quite banish the gloomy moods to which he was so subject. Even the necessity of staying in Paris again without any proper home— the Paris that he hated and that yet drew him back as with a spell, the city of so many troubles and toils, so many dreams and disappointments—was a constraint that embittered his soul.

Minna, who loved to be busy and bustling about, and was probably encouraged by von Lüttichau's kindness, hit on the idea of applying to the chief statesman of Saxony, the President of the Council and, at that time, Minister of the Interior, Baron von Beust, to use his influence on her husband's behalf.

As we mentioned above, all the prisoners of the May rising had been released, except one ; only Röckel was still in the Waldheim Prison, and the Dresden authorities were beginning to find this annoying, and wanted to get rid of the last man. It was intended to release him on the King's birthday, December 12, 1861—at least, he says so himself in his well-known book [1]— but the plan fell through, as Röckel's doctrinaire republicanism jibbed at consenting to a petition for pardon, even as a mere formality. In addition, Röckel's daughter Louisabeth [2] had been staying in Dresden since December 4, in order to plead for her father's pardon ; and, owing to the friendship between Wagner and Röckel, the latter's daughter naturally called on Frau Wagner, and thus Minna was fully informed as to the state of Röckel's affairs.[1]   All this may have led her to form the plan of working personally for her husband's amnesty, and thus carrying out the wish he expressed on November 13.   When she told him about the matter he wrote to her on December 21, 1861 :

> And now I have forgotten to answer you about Beust. I make up for the omission by giving you a free hand to do what you think best ; you must treat the business as if you were acting for yourself.   For my part I am not in the mood to bow down to the dust before them ! They are really quite too contemptible, and if they amnesty me they will do it not for my sake or yours, but half for shame—and because it has got to be done !

Hate, it is said, has keen sight ; in the course of years Wagner had realized, in spite of the soaring optimism that alternated in him with abysmal pessimism, that any understanding of his music, and a resultant personal interest in the composer, could only be found in Germany among individual men and women of high intellectual and spiritual quality.   He saw that, even among the so-called educated classes— ' good society,' quite apart from the masses—he sometimes met with hostility and generally with indifference, and that most of those who set the tone, the German Governments, were unfriendly to him.   Saxony especially, and its official and Court society, still kept to the fable of Wagner the revolutionary fanatic as an article of their political catechism.

But at last it dawned even on officials and courtiers that the man must be something more than a mere theatrical agitator or incendiary ; persons of princely rank, related to the Royal Family, had received him, distinguished him by their favour, even urgently interceded for him with Saxony, had been his patrons, or at least had shown him gracious consideration. Among these were Queen Victoria and Albert, Prince Consort, himself one of the Wettin family, and the Grand Dukes and Duchesses of Weimar and Baden, the Princess— by this time Queen—of Prussia, the Archduke who was Governor of Lombardy, and the Emperor Napoleon III. Was Saxony still to keep to its isolation—Saxony, where for years the Court Theatre had had to open its doors to Wagner's operas, since Saxony could not stay outside the world of European culture ?

Von Seebach was at his Saxon home in January 1862, but Wagner still hoped to meet him there again before he left Paris ; meanwhile Minna was to look him up at Dresden. " In any case he would be the best man to try. If this Saxon difficulty could be got over it would help everything." [1] Wagner spent January in Paris, and early in February he travelled to Mainz, finally settling in Biebrich, which is beautifully situated on the Rhine, half-way between Mainz and Wiesbaden. February and most of March were taken up with hard work, visits to the Grand Duke at Karlsruhe, plans for the future, and other business. In the meantime his wife had been busy at Dresden ; it was urged upon her to get Wagner again to present a petition for pardon, which would give an ostensible reason for granting the amnesty, so often asked for and as often refused. By this time the authorities were ready to be magnanimous, but would not take the first step.

While Wagner was installing his furniture, forwarded from Paris, at Biebrich, Minna arrived quite unexpectedly to help him put his house in order, and to arrange for sending her furniture on to Dresden. She was able to inform him that the plan he had often discussed before—that of having a room always ready for him in her house, as a harbour of refuge in his restless, roving life—could now be realized without difficulty if only he would present a petition to King John for form's sake. This suggestion, however, much annoyed the Master. We can see from his letter of March 11, 1862, that the days they spent together at Biebrich, in spite of the advantage of having her help (as he readily admits in his autobiography), were no pleasant and peaceful time for him. The old, miserable scenes of jealousy wearied and irritated him, and we gather the impression that life in Dresden gave rise to heated discussions.

Wagner had already humbled himself before King John, Crown Prince Albert, Behr, the Minister of Justice, and von Lüttichau, the General Manager, at the sacrifice of his strong sense of his own dignity; he had openly confessed his faults, and had pleaded for pardon in most pathetic terms, for the sake of his artistic aims; his pride as an artist and a man now revolted at the suggestion that he should sue for pardon as a penitent sinner. At the same time a suspicion arose in his mind, as it had in similar cases before, that his confession of his faults and petition for pardon would merely be used to inflict public humiliation on him. In any case, his wife, during her stay with him, could not induce him to write the hateful letter, and even afterward he had to be reminded by letter before, after some weeks, he forced himself to the task.

> To-morrow the letter to the King follows. I am not well, and in low spirits. . . . I thought, too, that I had already written enough to the King and his Ministers. Lately, as I see in the papers, several people have been allowed a free return—I hear from Köchly that he could have come back to Saxony last year without any trouble. So it is with very bitter feelings and great reluctance that I start on such a letter, which may only be used to inflict a public humiliation on me. You might very well tell the Minister that he might, for instance, remind the King of my letter of last summer, forwarded by Seebach.[1] I really don't know how to find the proper empty words ; it makes me miserable—I have torn up several drafts already. Why is there such a hurry for it ? Could not the permission to re-enter Saxony be simply considered as the long-expected answer to my countless petitions ?
> Well, perhaps I shall have a more amiable moment to-morrow. If I can draft out a short but sufficient formula you shall have it. . . . So good-bye for the present. Thanks for your kindness. All will come right —only I am rather hard to please just now.

He might well have felt that this time he was wronging Minna, even if she had worried him by her persistency, for she was carrying out his instructions by pleading his cause at Dresden. But the "amiable moment" did not come "to-morrow"; it was not till the 25th that he wrote the following petition :

> MOST AUGUST KING,
> MOST SERENE KING AND LORD,
> I have to thank your Majesty's grace for having been allowed for two years to enter the states of the Confederation, and my artistic endeavours have benefited by this access to the chief German theatres. Unfortunately, one of the best and finest of these, your Majesty's Court

Theatre at Dresden, is still beyond my reach, and thus one of the fairest fields for my art is closed to me.

Furthermore, it is plain to me that my home interests are most seriously prejudiced so long as Dresden is inaccessible to me. My wife, who has shared the vicissitudes of exile with me for thirteen years, requires a settled home, in order to enjoy the rest necessary for her impaired health and her serious heart trouble; this she feels she can find only in Dresden, which has been her home from her youth and where she wishes to stay for the rest of her life.

It is this consideration, and my earnest wish to obtain for my poor wife, so sorely tried, the refuge she desires for the rest of her days, that have moved me to apply to your Majesty in a humble petition that it may be your august pleasure to grant me full amnesty and a free return to my native land.

In support of my humble request I venture to appeal to the testimony of my friend Dr Anton Pusinelli, of Dresden, which he is ready to give if requested. He has attended my wife for the last four years during her repeated visits to her home.

With absolute trust in your Majesty's gracious clemency, and with the promise ever to show myself by my conduct worthy of the grace of my august King and Lord, I remain, humbly and in loyal submission,

Your Majesty's most obedient subject,

RICHARD WAGNER

BIEBRICH (ON THE RHINE)
March, 25, 1862

Annexed to the petition was the medical report of his old friend and family physician, Dr Pusinelli, which is worth notice for its minute information as to the state of Minna's health; for it was in part due to her malady that her temperament was a torture to herself and her husband—torture that Wagner bore for many years. The report shows that Minna was the victim of her physical condition, and gives us the key to the

Master's long, self-sacrificing consideration for her; this cannot be disputed, in spite of his occasional irritability and harshness, and his letters to Minna give eloquent proof of it.   Pusinelli writes : [1]

> Being requested by the wife of Kapellmeister Wagner to draw up a report on her state of health, I do so as follows, truly and as in duty bound.
>
> During the years 1843–49, as family physician to the Wagner family, I had occasion to observe the excellent health and robust constitution of Frau Wagner until her departure from Dresden.   During her subsequent stay at Zürich vague reports reached me now and then of her ill-health, but it was not till 1858, during her stay in Dresden, where she had come for the restoration of her health, that I was able to convince myself of the truth of these reports.   I own that I was greatly shocked by my first sight of a woman who was once so strong and healthy.   I had not expected to see such a remarkable change in her whole outward appearance, such startling evidence of acute internal trouble.   The examination which I made unfortunately confirmed the truth of my first impression, that her health was shattered.   I found signs of organic heart disease, an irregular pulse, continual breathlessness, a trembling voice, an anxious, frightened expression on her pale face, a continual, uncontrollable restlessness.   These and other symptoms confirmed my diagnosis ; . . . so that her condition at the time appeared almost hopeless.   However, the treatment I at once employed, as to medicine and diet, together with a subsequent cure at Schandau, was most successful, and considerably abated the symptoms—all the more because the stay in her native land had a beneficial effect on the patient's mind.   I was unable, however, to effect a complete cure. It was with apprehension that I saw my patient in the autumn of 1858, at her husband's summons, leave here again against my advice, and exchange the beneficial quiet of her residence here for the excitement of Paris life.[2] The consequences were as I feared.   The reports which I received from her were not reassuring, and betrayed

her longing to return home. After two summers of suffering my patient finally returned here in the autumn of 1861. The good effects of her former stay in Dresden had almost entirely vanished, and it needed speedy attention and drastic treatment to restore the tolerable conditions of 1858. Since then the disease has made no progress, there has been no further enlargement of the heart, and thus all that is possible has been done. Although there is no hope of a complete cure, the disease is checked ; but, in order to make this check permanent, it is requisite that the patient should live under favourable conditions, and avoid those hurtful influences which caused her trouble. Among these latter agitation of mind comes first. No other organ of the body is so definitely and permanently affected by mental troubles as the heart, and just as the agitations from which Frau Wagner suffered in 1849 were the first cause of her present disease, so the continual grief and longing for home that beset her during the subsequent period were the sources from which her complaint derived its growth. If the present improvement in her health is to be permanent it is indispensable that she should be able to stay quietly in her native country, under continual medical supervision. For, after the bad effects of ceaseless hurrying to and fro, home-sickness, ever gnawing at the heart, is the most dangerous enemy to health, and its slow but sure poison must undermine even the strongest constitution, and inevitably ruin an organ that is already diseased. As a physician, I am bound to give it as my decided opinion that Frau Wagner should stay quietly in Dresden, so that the recent improvement in her condition may be lasting, and that any change for the worse, which would otherwise be inevitable, may be prevented.

DR ANTON PUSINELLI
*Practising Physician, and Surgeon
to the Royal Hospital*

DRESDEN
March, 25, 1862

The immediate success of this petition showed that the Dresden authorities had only been waiting for

Wagner's formal application, for the necessary measures were taken forthwith. The medical certificate made things easier, for the amnesty to Wagner looked also like an act of grace to his sick wife.

Wagner's letter cannot have reached Dresden before March 26, and there is no endorsement on it of the date when it was received in the office ; but at the top of the first page, in the King's own handwriting, are pencilled the few but significant words, " Wagner is to have free entry." This decision was probably taken on March 27, for on March 28 a minute of the official permit was drawn up in the office of the Ministry of Justice, to which the letter had been handed. This was initialled on the 29th by the King and the Minister of Justice, von Behr. Von Behr wrote in pencil on the margin, " Can be handed to his wife, who lives here." On March 31 the fair copy was made, and it was sent to Minna on April 1.

ANSWER [1]

To the former Kapellmeister, Herr Richard Wagner, now at Biebrich-on-Rhine

His Majesty the King, in answer to the petition for pardon presented directly by you, is pleased to exempt you from any further prosecution on account of your participation in the treasonable enterprise of May 1849, and the criminal proceedings therewith connected, and to grant you the right of free re-entry into Saxony. The necessary instructions will forthwith be given to the District Court charged with the inquiry, whereof you will be duly informed.

THE MINISTRY OF JUSTICE

Dresden
March 28, 1862

L

At the same time the Ministry of Justice drew up the instruction to the Dresden District Court, signifying to it, as the tribunal charged with the prosecution of Wagner, his full amnesty and permission to return freely.   On April 3 Wagner had not yet received this answer, and meanwhile must have had another complaining letter from Minna, which greatly annoyed him.   He writes to her that all his thoughts must now be concentrated on his new opera—everything else is a matter of indifference.   He would have been thankful to get the news of his amnesty after wasting his time at Vienna, and to hear that a quiet place to work in was ready for him in Dresden.   Now all this unsettles him, for money difficulties prevent him from finding such a place.   What good was Dresden now?   All his hopes rested on prospects outside Saxony.

This amnesty, which has been so terribly long in coming—what is it worth to me under present conditions? I will admit that last winter, when Bürde was still at her best,[1] it might have been of great service to me to get the Dresden Theatre and Tichatschek for *Tristan*.   I shall hope to get the opera done there in its complete form, and I confess that it is worth while for me, as an artist, to have Dresden open to me again. . . . Further, it is well that the amnesty has removed the stigma which up till now . . . would have kept certain high and mighty personages from having anything to do with me. If the amnesty had arrived last year I could have gone to Berlin in the winter and tried my luck at Court. . . .[2] I had only one real and pressing reason for writing to the King again, and that was my anxiety for you, for I knew that only in Dresden would you find a settled home for life.[3]   For my part, I find it very hard to accept the plan of settling in Dresden again, and I should prefer any other place where I can be quite by myself. . . .   I will see to my letter of thanks as soon as the regular official notice comes as an answer to my letter; I have always got their negative answers in due course, so I suppose they will send me the affirmative this time.

In point of fact, the favourable answer soon arrived, for on April 9 Wagner sent his acknowledgment to Minna: "Here is the letter for the Minister, in which I express my thanks and request him to lay my duty at his Majesty's feet!" The letter is addressed to von Behr, as the note in his handwriting on Wagner's letter, "Put with the papers on Wagner's amnesty. V. B.," shows.

YOUR EXCELLENCY,

It is to your kind recommendation that I undoubtedly in great part owe the acceptance of the petition that I lately addressed to his Majesty. I therefore express to you my most grateful thanks for the fact that, as I have been informed, I can freely return to Saxony.

As I can now consider the possibility of definitely settling in Dresden next autumn, it only remains for me to make my humble and sincere request to your Excellency kindly to offer to his Majesty my warmest thanks for the great favour shown to me, and the assurance of the faith and fealty to which I am pledged for all future time.

I remain, with the greatest respect and esteem,
Your Excellency's obedient servant,
RICHARD WAGNER

BIEBRICH-ON-RHINE
April 9, 1862

We have already mentioned with what indifference Wagner expressed himself in writing to Minna, even before he received the notification of his amnesty, though he was sure that it was on the way. He preserved this cold, almost hostile attitude after he had the official notice of his full pardon ; he spoke as if the whole business did not concern him, but was rather Minna's affair.

" My wife has now succeeded in getting me a full amnesty from Dresden," he wrote to Röckel on April 5 ; " I am fixed here, where I am quite comfortable, and find it beautifully quiet for work."   This indifference was doubtless largely due to Minna's eagerness to take up her quarters in Dresden, counting on his making a long stay there ; but Wagner, after long and patient endurance of her jealous, suspicious temperament, had made up his mind that he would provide for her comfort, and occasionally pay her short visits, but never stay with her for long—much less as a permanence.   If they lived together for any length of time both of them would be worn out with ceaseless quarrels.   As early as April 21 he warns his wife that he has various engagements elsewhere, so that he cannot be continually in Dresden ; he coolly leaves it to her to arrange her quarters as she chooses.

> I am still in doubt how far Dresden can prove a comfortable residence for me ; I dare say I shall find out. My only reason for choosing Dresden is that I know you are happiest there, and prefer it to any other home.

Later on too he absolutely refuses to bind himself down to Dresden as a permanent residence.

VIII

WAGNER'S VISIT TO DRESDEN
CONCLUSION

AT the end of October 1862 Wagner travelled *via* Leipzig to Dresden, where he arrived on November 3, and stayed with Minna until the 6th. Thirteen and a half years had gone by since his flight from the city on May 9, 1849, before he was permitted to walk the familiar streets again. No mournful memories were awakened in his mind : his resentment was too deep at what he considered the undeserved harshness of the Saxon King and Government and of the Theatre management. He was surprised at the quiet of the streets—there still hovered before his eyes a vision of the stormy days of the Revolution—and he was saddened by the thought of so many old friends who were no longer there. However, he thought it proper to call on the Minister of Justice, von Behr, as the official immediately concerned with his amnesty, and on the President of the Council, von Beust. We have a short account of this in his autobiography, and a description in von Beust's memoirs.

As to von Behr, Wagner tells us how that too apprehensive Minister, although he had signed the amnesty, declared that he still feared lest the composer's popularity might give rise to undesirable demonstrations. Wagner partially reassured him by declaring that he was only making a short stay in Dresden, and had no intention of going to the theatre, and the Minister dismissed him with a sigh and a frown. Von Beust, on the contrary, greeted him with smiling courtesy, and remarked that Wagner was not such an innocent as he made out, alluding to a letter of Wagner's which had been found in Röckel's pocket. But he readily agreed that the amnesty must be accepted as an absolution for all past errors. The two parted on the most friendly terms. The description gives us the impression that both were playing a part in this interview.[1]

Von Beust, in his memoirs, gives a very different account of what took place.[2] He first attributes Wagner's pardon to Tichatschek's intercession. We have already seen that Tichatschek had tried to bring about an understanding through von Lüttichau; but, as regards the final settlement, there is no trace either in the documents or in Wagner's correspondence of any effective action on the part of his old friend Tscheckel. Von Beust says that, on the occasion of Wagner's visit, he began by expressing to the composer the satisfaction he felt at having been able to do anything for him, and a hope that he would not give him trouble by any further demonstrations.[3] Wagner's strange answer, " I don't understand you," led him to allude to 1849, whereupon Wagner characterized the events of that time as an unfortunate misunderstanding. Von Beust countered this excuse (he says) with the remark that in the archives there was a letter written by Wagner in which he boasted of the attempt—fortunately unsuccessful—to set fire to the Royal Palace.

This latter statement must be put down as wanton misrepresentation. We must reject the idea that von Beust deliberately made up this fable; we can see,

FRIEDRICH FERDINAND, BARON VON BEUST, SAXON MINISTER
FOR FOREIGN AFFAIRS

From a lithograph by F. Zöllern (1852), inscribed, " Painted from life by
Professor Vogel von Vogelstein, 1852."

Municipal Museum, Dresden   166

however, how inaccurate his other statements are on important points that can be definitely determined, and this makes it easier to treat this story, entirely unsupported by any evidence, as what it was—a mistake, a slip of the memory, probably due to the interval of twenty-four years (1862–86) or even thirty-seven years (1849–86) between the events and the compiling of von Beust's memoirs. No such letter can be found in the archives. When Wagner petitioned for pardon in 1856 the charges against him were collected, and all the other indictments were searched for anything that could throw light, or shadow, on his actions in 1849, but nobody knew anything about this monstrous charge, and not the slightest reference was made to anything of the sort. Thus we cannot go wrong in supposing that in the actual interview von Beust did not speak definitely of any letter of Wagner's in which he boasted of setting fire to the palace, but only referred in general terms to some letter that seriously compromised Wagner. Wagner would hardly have left such a charge unanswered, or would at least have mentioned it indignantly in his autobiography. When he wrote this work (1865) he had no notion of the charge brought by von Beust, which was first published in 1887, so he had no occasion to give an innocent explanation of the supposed document. He naturally interpreted von Beust's remark as referring to the well-known letter that he wrote to Röckel at Prague on May 2, 1849, which certainly revealed him as a fellow-conspirator, but by no means as an incendiary; this letter is actually in the archives to this day. It is possible that, during the long interval between 1849 and 1862, there had been some malicious gossip on the subject in Court and official circles. The slanders circulated, as Wagner complains, by the Saxon Ambassador at Vienna included silly stories about incendiarism; but there was no foundation for these rumours, as we shall see presently.

The Master's economic position was not improved, in spite of his unrestricted intercourse with Germany and his freedom to go about there; various attempts to organize either performances of his operas or concerts only brought him fresh disappointments, and even an increase of his embarrassments, in return for his labour and trouble. He grew embittered, and now and then vented his bitterness with especial force against Saxony and Dresden. He had the fixed idea that an earlier amnesty would have offered far better prospects and opportunities of bringing his new works into public notice, and thus assuring his own position.

From February to April 1863 he was in Russia, where his reception filled him with hopes of success and substantial profit. These brighter prospects made him feel the contrast between his own country and foreign lands still more painfully, and he breaks out in a letter to Minna of March 5 :

It is a strange thing that here in Russia I should find the help that I ought to have found in Germany. And what about Saxony, dear Saxony, good, kind Leipzig, and dear, noble Dresden, where I was treated like a mangy cat ! . . . I feel so bitter that I am beginning to find it funny. Has my lawyer, Schmidt, told you what was in my letter to him ? . . . And all the scandalous intrigues of the Saxon Ambassador, even at Vienna, where Herr K[önneritz] is always telling everybody how I set fire to the Royal Palace ! [1] Ah, how gratifying it is to have the love and sympathy of one's own dear fatherland !

The amusement he affected to find in these annoyances was not very genuine ; we can see from his autobiography, written some years later, how deeply he was hurt by this slanderous story of incendiarism. In describing his failure at Vienna he explains the fruitlessness of his efforts to gain the favour of the Imperial Family by the fact that

> a member of the Könneritz family, which seems to crop up everywhere as a stumbling-block in my path, was then Ambassador there, and managed to check any tendency to favour me on the part of the all-powerful Archduchess Sophie by declaring that in his time I had burned down the King of Saxony's palace.

Sophie, the mother of the Emperor Francis Joseph, was the sister of Queen Amalie * and twin sister of the Queen-Dowager Marie of Saxony.   It is obvious that Sophie took the side of her sisters and the Saxon Royal Family, and cherished a natural prejudice against the revolutionary party, but, in view of the close relations between the sisters and their constant correspondence, such a downright lie on the part of the Ambassador would have been flatly impossible ; and even among Court circles generally Könneritz would have found no credit for this particular slander which Wagner ascribes to him.   All he did was to repeat, without troubling to verify them, the stories current about Wagner in Dresden Society, and that was probably enough to discredit Wagner with Vienna Court circles, except in the case of the young Empress Elizabeth, who

* Consort of King John of Saxony.—TRANSLATOR.

was uninfluenced by such stories and was in the habit
of going to his concerts alone. There is no other
proof that the von Könneritz family was always hostile
to Wagner: Marie von Könneritz was one of his most
enthusiastic partisans in the forties. How little the
Royal Family believed these exaggerated reports is
shown—apart from the absence of any documentary
reference—by King John's silence on the question in
his letters to the Grand Dukes of Baden and Weimar,
in which he speaks severely of Wagner's conduct, and
singles out as especially criminal in a Court *employé* his
stirring up sedition among the orchestra. While the
King was on this topic an alleged attempt to burn
down the residence of the Royal Family would have
been far more deadly to Wagner's reputation, but his
Majesty says not a word about it.

When Wagner wrote the scornful words we have
quoted about Saxony and Dresden he was far from
being so amused as he made out. His resentment at
these false charges was so strong that the letter to his
lawyer, Schmidt, which he mentioned to Minna is
nothing less than a request to Schmidt to apply to the
Dresden District Court for permission to consult the
documents relating to the revolution of May 1849, so
as to prove the falsehood of this report. The papers
dealing with Wagner's share in the rebellion, first
collected in 1856, bear the official endorsement that
Schmidt produced a letter from Wagner as his authorization, and this was considered sufficient. Wagner's
actual letter is not filed with the papers, as it contained
other matter which was private. The document
Schmidt, as Wagner's legal representative, drew up

was found among Schmidt's papers, and in 1881 was placed in the Royal Public Library, now the State Library.

In his letter from Berlin of February 20, 1863, Wagner instructs his lawyer to settle a dispute with the bookseller Arnold, and, further, to make extracts of the heads of accusation against Wagner for his share in the May revolt. He says he has been advised by friends in high position (possibly von Seebach) to use these extracts to refute the slanders about his incendiarism, and, if necessary, to institute a regular inquiry; perhaps Schmidt could come to an understanding with von Beust on the matter.

> In the interview which he granted me last November at Dresden I took occasion to make an urgent request that he would satisfy the Government of the Duke of Saxe-Weimar (who was friendly toward me) by a suitable declaration that, if the latter decided to take me into his service in any capacity, it would not be regarded as an offence to the Saxon Court. Herr von Beust solemnly promised me to speak to his Majesty on the subject ; but I hear from Weimar that no satisfactory declaration of the kind has reached von Watzdorf, the Minister there, and I must infer, from several indications, that the Weimar Court are still apprehensive on that point. It would be very kind and helpful if you could induce Herr von Beust to intervene in my name, and put matters straight.

In consequence of this letter Schmidt, on March 21, 1863, addressed the necessary request to the Dresden District Court.

> Herr Richard Wagner, formerly Royal Kapellmeister, has been hindered in his efforts to establish a secure and suitable position in Germany by the insinuations, circulated in influential quarters, that during the revolt at Dresden in May 1849 he made, and was charged with

making, an attempt to set fire to the Royal Palace. Herr Wagner is, of course, guiltless of having made any such criminal attempt, or of even having thought of doing so, and can well afford to ignore such a charge, seeing that his Majesty has graciously granted him the right of free return to the Kingdom of Saxony. But since the report is likely to cause him permanent damage, and to endanger his peace and his position, he has requested me to inspect the documents [1] relating to the May rising at Dresden, and to verify whether the above-mentioned insinuation rests on any positive evidence, and especially whether the depositions of the witnesses point to any such conduct on the part of Herr Wagner, and on the basis of the results of the inquiry to take further steps either seriously to refute these malicious slanders or to demonstrate the baselessness of their origin.

He therefore asks in Wagner's name for the papers relating to Wagner to be delivered to him at his house and to be left for a few days, or, if this is not convenient, for leave to inspect them at the court. On March 23 the papers were left at his house for eight days. Schmidt made extracts from the documents, and put the results of his inquiry into the form of a certificate, which he sent in June 1863 to Wagner. In this the charges given in the first chapter of the present work are briefly mentioned. At the end of the indictment it is expressly stated :

> Especially, in no place is even a suggestion to be seen that Herr Wagner made an attempt or formed a plan to set fire to the Royal Palace at Dresden or any other public or private building.

So, at the close of the fateful period of Wagner's exile, from 1849 to 1862, comes an echo from the event in his life which was the origin of that sorrowful time, the revolution of May.

Wagner's further relations with Dresden lie outside the limits of the present narrative. We may only add to it an account of an event of later date, relating to a matter that repeatedly exercised him during his exile and enters into his letters about his amnesty—the settlement of the old loan of 1848.

Wagner occasionally adopted the point of view that this affair was dead and done with, but his offers to work off the debt in exchange for his musical services show that he himself believed that he still owed the money. When he received a full pardon this matter does not seem to have been discussed, but the management had not forgotten it, though it did not come up for decision till after Wagner's death.

When, just a year after the Master's death, Frau Cosima made a contract (on February 25, confirmed on March 6, 1884) with the management of the royal orchestra and the Court Theatre, Dresden, for herself and her son Siegfried, through her representative at Bayreuth, Councillor Gross, giving Dresden the right to produce *Tristan* and the *Nibelung* series, the question of the long-outstanding debt was settled by the decision of the Saxon management to renounce its claim. Clause 8 reads :

> In case the above contract becomes legally binding on both parties, the General Management of the Court Theatre, in virtue of the powers granted to it, shall give up all claim for the repayment of the loan of 5000 thalers (15,000 marks) made to the late Richard Wagner from the Pension Fund of the Court Theatre.

Thus, after more than thirty years, this troublesome affair was peaceably settled ; and the works written during Wagner's exile were at last available for performance in the theatre which, forty years before, had been the first in Germany to open its doors to one of his important operas, thus enabling the composer to take his first step on the upward path to fame and fortune.

APPENDIX

MINOR CONTRIBUTIONS TO THE HISTORY OF WAGNER AND HIS WORKS

I

THE MANAGEMENT OF THE DRESDEN THEATRE AND WAGNER'S WORKS (1854–56)

IN the course of this narrative we have mentioned that during the time, in the middle of the fifties, when the Dresden Government was flatly refusing to entertain any petition for Wagner's pardon, and even his operas, after a passing revival of *Tannhäuser* in 1852, were excluded from the Court Theatre —when, so to speak, politically, legally, and socially his existence was ignored—the theatrical management was far less unapproachable and implacable.

Whenever anyone applied to the Dresden management with reference to Wagner's music with any request that could be complied with, it was readily granted ; there was never any sign of petty hostility, deliberate spitefulness, or even disinclination to handle his compositions. They were even careful not to deal with his work without his knowledge or to disregard his rights ; in cases where his consent was required they always referred inquirers to him, and did not comply with the request till they had his authorization. It is worth noticing that this was not done in the ordinary routine of the office, but under the express directions of the 'wicked' von Lüttichau.

The following illustrative cases are taken from the archives of the Saxon State Theatre, formerly the Court Theatre, from the " Papers relating to Manuscripts and Scores " for the years 1854–56.

A. Woltersdorff, manager of the Town Theatre at Königs-berg, wrote from there on February 21, 1854, to the General Manager, von Lüttichau :

175

Fräulein Johanna Wagner, who is giving a season here this spring, wishes, as part of her programme, to sing *Iphigénie en Aulide* in the version prepared by her uncle for the Saxon Court Theatre. I would ask your Excellency kindly to lend me the score and libretto of this opera from the Royal Library for about a fortnight, so that I may arrange my score from it.

On the same day that this request reached Dresden von Lüttichau made the memorandum, "February 24. Decline; must apply to Wagner himself." On the next day the answer was sent from the office to Königsberg :

SIR,
I have to state on behalf of his Excellency, in answer to your letter of the 21st inst., that we regret we cannot comply with your wish for the loan of the version of Gluck's *Iphigénie en Aulide* prepared by the former Kapellmeister Wagner for the Court Theatre here, seeing that this version was specially arranged and intended for this theatre, and consequently cannot be sent anywhere else without the composer's express permission.

DRESDEN
February 25, 1854

Woltersdorff at once applied to Wagner, who readily consented.

DEAR SIR,
Excuse me for having troubled you with unnecessary questions; I was misled by an erroneous report (which came from Herr von Hülsen himself). I shall be glad to allow you the use of my arrangement of Gluck's *Iphigénie en Aulide*. Will you kindly show this note to Herr von Lüttichau in authorization ?

With all respect,
Yours sincerely,
RICHARD WAGNER

ZÜRICH
April 17, 1854

The Königsberg manager sent this letter, in the original, to the Dresden management, who filed it among their papers for reference, and made no further objection to complying with his request. They wrote to him :

As we have received Herr Richard Wagner's authorization from Zürich, there is no longer any difficulty in the way of lending you the score of *Iphigénie en Aulide* as arranged by him. We are sending it, with the libretto, and shall expect it to be returned in a fortnight's time, according to promise.

I remain, etc.

· · · · ·

DRESDEN
April 29, 1854

When the parcel arrived at Königsberg on May 4 it was found that they would have to copy out the solo and chorus parts for use there; there was no time to get out the orchestral parts. So Woltersdorff (in a letter written on May 5 to the Assistant Manager, Karl Theodor Winkler) asked if he could have these also sent from Dresden, " for Fräulein Johanna Wagner's season, this month," and the Dresden management again, on May 8, complied with his request.

The next year Woltersdorff repeated his application. On April 30, 1855, he wrote to Winkler that last year the opera arrived so late that Johanna Wagner could only appear in it once; consequently he was now asking to have Wagner's score and orchestral parts again for three or four weeks. The reply came by return, on May 5, that von Lüttichau had granted his request " on the spot."

The same readiness was shown in other cases. On June 20, 1854, Wangenheim, the head of the ducal orchestra and theatrical management at Coburg, wrote to Dresden that he wanted " to stage Wagner's opera *Tannhäuser* during the next autumn season," and had had sketches made for the costumes. " But since it is well known that the production of that opera is nowhere so fine as at the Royal Court Theatre at Dresden," he asked to have a look at the Dresden sketches for the scenery and costumes. On June 28 three coloured sketches of the grotto of Venus, the gate of the Wartburg, and the Hall of the Minnesingers, three ground-plans, and sixteen sheets of costume sketches were sent to Coburg. We know that Wagner had a considerable share in the technical production of the piece, and von Lüttichau may have felt additional pleasure in the fact that the fine production which Wagner had organized found acceptance elsewhere.

When Franz Rothmayer, the manager of the Town Theatre at Hamburg, on November 2, 1854, wished to perform, at a celebration of Schiller's birthday, " the overture to *Iphigénie en Aulide*, as rescored by Richard Wagner," and asked for the score and orchestral parts of Act I, von Lüttichau refused, but not as a matter of principle; he merely said that " these particular compositions of Richard Wagner cannot be parted with."

When the General Manager at Berlin, von Hülsen, was giving a concert for the sufferers from inundations in Silesia, and telegraphed, on December 1, 1854, for the loan of the orchestral parts of *Tannhäuser*, they were sent off at once to Berlin on December 2, with a request for their return as soon as possible, " since we want them here." On December 11 von Hülsen returned them with thanks.

Von Lüttichau displayed the same caution as in the case of Woltersdorff in 1854 when, on April 20, 1856, the Grand Ducal Theatre at Weimar wanted to borrow " as soon as possible, for a few days, the solo vocal parts of the opera *Iphigénie en Aulide*, in Wagner's arrangement." His answer was :

DEAR SIR,
    On receipt of your letter I at once laid it before his Excellency. He regrets that he cannot immediately comply with your wish, but considers it necessary in this case that Herr Richard Wagner should first be asked to give his authorization. On receipt of the desired permission the parts in question shall be forwarded at once.

                    With all respect,
                        I remain, dear sir,

                                            . . . . .

DRESDEN
    April 21, 1856

A headmaster at Döbeln, Karl Gustav Schubert, who had for years given performances at his school on the birthday of King Frederick Augustus, desired in 1854 to heighten the interest by a musical celebration. He explained this in a long letter to von Lüttichau (April 18, 1854), and went on to say :

For this purpose I now need a piece of music that, I imagine, can only be found in the archives of the royal orchestra. I mean the Festival Ode which the former Kapellmeister Wagner wrote and composed for the return of our sovereign from England, which was sung one morning in the garden at Pillnitz.

He goes on to ask for the vocal and orchestral parts, as he wishes " to provide the music with a suitable text, to the best of my ability, in the hope that my words will find an echo in the hearts of all who hear them."

The piece he referred to was the song of welcome, *Gruss seiner Treuen an König Friedrich August den Geliebten*, written, composed, and rehearsed in two days, and offered by Wagner to the King on his return from abroad on the morning of August 12, 1844. The loyal von Lüttichau may have thought it an ominous choice to select this royalist piece by one who was afterward to be notorious as a rebel ; still, he showed no reluctance or misgiving, and wrote most obligingly :

His Excellency would send you with pleasure the composition by Wagner which you want if it were in the musical archives of the Royal Theatre, but it was never deposited there by Wagner. However, I hear that it was published by Möser [1] here a long time ago, not in the full score, but in a vocal and piano arrangement.

I remain, etc.

. . . . .

DRESDEN
April 29, 1854

Thus, even when he could do nothing himself, he was still solicitous for Wagner's interests.

These separate instances taken from the years 1854-56 are enough to prove that, in spite of the stiffly hostile attitude of the Government, the theatrical management, in questions concerning music only, showed no animosity against Wagner, and was scrupulously correct in dealing with him. From Wagner's letters to Fischer we learn, too, that when Wagner asked for a copy of the score of his arrangement of *Iphigénie en Aulide* from Dresden, von Lüttichau complied with his request, though he took rather a long time about it.

179

II

WAGNER AND KÖCHLY

A famous name among the revolutionists of May at
Dresden is that of the classical philologist and lecturer at
the Kreuzschule, Hermann Köchly (1815–76). He was
then a deputy in the Saxon Diet, and a member of a com-
mittee preparing a new Education Act, the draft of which
was chiefly his work. From 1842 onward he was Latin
tutor to Princes Ernest and George, the younger sons of
Prince John. Ernest died young in 1847, but George,
afterward King of Saxony (1902–4), remained his pupil
and was largely indebted for his excellent education to
Köchly's faculty of vividly portraying the spirit of antiquity.
The tuition went on till just before the outbreak of the
revolution. On May 20, 1849, Prince John wrote from
the Königstein to his eldest son, Albert, who was then
with the Saxon troops in Schleswig :

FORTRESS OF KÖNIGSTEIN
May 20, 1849

No fresh arrests of any importance have been made.
Warrants have lately been issued against Wagner and the two
editors of the *Dresdner Zeitung*. Köchly is supposed to be
the man who proclaimed the Provisional Government to the
people; but he seems to have got away in time. Semper too
is over the hills and far away. Nothing is known of Todt
and Tschirner; it is said they are at Frankfurt, but as there is
nothing about it in any paper, I fancy the report is put about
to throw people off the scent.

YOUR LOVING PAPA

In his next letter John gives further details :

FORTRESS OF KÖNIGSTEIN
May 25, 1849

There is no more news here, except that a warrant is out
against friend Köchly. He gave George a lesson as late as
May 2, and wanted to arrange for a third lesson that week—
at the same time he seems to have been very brusque and
ungracious.

As Köchly expected to give a third lesson that same week after May 2, which was a Wednesday, it is clear that he himself was surprised by the outbreak of the revolution on May 3. He fled *via* Hamburg to Brussels, whence he was called to the chair of Classical Philology at the University of Zürich, where he took up his post at Easter 1850.

Köchly found many Saxon refugees at Zürich, among others Privy Councillor Todt, the lecturer Marschall von Bieberstein, Richard Wagner, Tschirner, and, later on, Semper. He had a high position at Zürich, and in 1856 became Rector of the university. His relations with friends of Wagner's such as Georg Herwegh, Sulzer, and the Wesendonk and Wille families led to frequent meetings with Wagner, but no intimate friendship developed between either the two men or their wives. Wagner, in writing of the years at Zürich, only mentions Köchly once in his autobiography—in connexion with the occasion when Liszt and his friend Princess Caroline Wittgenstein stayed at Zürich in 1856, and annoyed Wagner by associating with the professors. Köchly, who was not musical, did not care for the style of Wagner's later operas ; he made a characteristic note in his diary about a *soirée* at Wesendonk's—" Quite tolerable, except for Wagner's stuff."

Apart from the divergence of their artistic doctrines, the two refugees were entire opposites in their views of life. While Wagner completely broke with his republican past, abandoned every form of political activity, and had as little as possible to do with his Saxon fellow-exiles,[1] Köchly, though he abstained from taking an active part in the cause of revolution and devoted himself entirely to his academic duties and his own special studies, remained true to his democratic views.[2]

In Köchly's letters (those that are in the State archives) to Schwender, his friend at Dresden, other refugees are often referred to, but of Wagner he speaks once only, in a letter of 1855. Schwender, who was an ardent collector of autographs, had asked Köchly to get him the signatures of well-known men at Zürich, Wagner among them. Köchly refers to this. We give the letter in full, for, apart from the passage about Wagner, it gives an interesting picture of conditions at Zürich.

MY DEAR FRIEND,

I take the opportunity offered by the kindness of Frau Klepperbein[1] to give you my best thanks for your charming letter of November last, and to assure you that it warmed my very heart. You may be sure that, in spite of my silence and my seclusion, my memories of dear old friends at Dresden, and the unforgettable days I spent there, are still fresh and lively, all the more that I have passed the age and the habit of mind that can make new friends. My longing for those past years would give me no rest if I could not say to myself that under present conditions such a life, or anything like it, would be impossible at Dresden. Much as my thoughts love to dwell with thankful emotion on the picture of a long, happy record of work together, I still thank my fate daily for having spared me the grief of seeing with my own eyes the downfall of the good cause, the ill-treatment and ruin of many of my friends, the triumph of a despicable reaction in State, church, and school.

There is not much to say about my life here. If you will apply to Frau Klepperbein she will (as she promised me) gladly give you all possible details, though she will not find it easy, owing to the extreme simplicity of my—I mean *our*—life here.

We live very quietly, and, outside of a little dramatic circle, which includes the former Fräulein Bauer, now Countess Plater, do not see much society. We keep out of the forced sociability of the Germans here, which I detest, but we are at home every evening to those few acquaintances who care to come in for a cup of tea. Besides this, I belong to one or two learned societies, mostly Swiss—*voilà tout*. My academical and classical work, which I thoroughly enjoy, fills up all the rest of my time, and I have grown into a stout and staid old fellow. I have resigned myself not to expect anything from Germany, and have given up the sanguine views that so many refugees still cherish; but, in spite of, or, rather, because of that, I am at peace with myself.

My wife, who, I hope, will present me with an addition to my family this month, is very well. She shares my taste for retirement. The twins are getting on finely. In short, my contentment with the little circle to which I have learned to limit my desires and hopes grows in proportion to my ever-growing hatred of the iniquities that once I strove against with all the fire and confidence of youth. Believe me, in spite of my present calm, I should be even less tolerant of the strait-jacket of monarchical rule than I was before. Here one sees for the first time how real republicanism, though with a touch of materialism, develops self-respect and character in men. My children shall be Swiss, unless—as I hardly expect—things get better in Germany. But enough about myself! Though I am a good deal changed, you will find me still the same old friend, but we must have a good talk before you will believe that, so do come and see us !

I have broken off all association with R. Wagner, so I can-not help you there. He has formed a little clique here of half a dozen people, who make an idol of him, adore his arrogance and rudeness (which, between ourselves, I consider is more affected than natural), and, what is very useful, occasionally pay his debts. It is my way to treat anyone I meet as an equal, not to put myself above him and certainly not below him ; so I could never stand such humbug, even if it did not bore me so. Wagner himself has thrown over his *Rienzi*, of which I still cherish enthusiastic memories, and wants to serve up instead his sloppy (excuse the word !) Christian-Romantic *Tannhäuser*, which I—you know it was always a bone of contention between us—find just as dull here, in spite of a very successful performance, as I did at Dresden.

However, I think I can get you the autographs of some Swiss celebrities ; only write down the names of those you want.

My Manetho has a Latin preface ; but the best parts of that have been cut out by the Paris censorship—I mean the censor-ship of my friend Dübner.[1]

My sister is at Berlin, and quite well. I hope your family are better now ; let me assure you of my deepest sympathy. Kind regards to all friends and acquaintances who remember me, especially Diethe, Leupold, Sachse, Reinicke, and Pfützner if they do remember me—I can hardly expect it. We refugees are really dead to our home, and whatever sound from us may reach your ears is like a ghostly voice from beyond the grave. Hearty greetings. Write again soon.

Most sincerely yours,
H. KÖCHLY

ZÜRICH
April 6, 1855

N.B.—Don't forget to give me your address.

Wagner's statement (see p. 157) that Köchly could have

easily come back to Saxony "last year" (*i.e.*, 1861) was quite wrong. Köchly refused to present a petition for pardon to King John, who, he was told, thought highly of him as his sons' tutor. "King John and I are a pig-headed pair, and I won't do it," he said, and the mediation of friends at Dresden was in vain. However, Köchly went to Germany in 1861, and attended the Philological Congress at Frankfort-on-the-Main after the Saxon envoy at the Diet had promised to ignore his presence. Then he went on to Bonn and Berlin, without having been formally amnestied by Saxony. It was not until 1862, when he was offered the headship of the celebrated college at Hamburg, the Johanneum, that the Hamburg authorities applied to the Saxon Government. Von Beust asked (June 12, 1862) the Minister of Justice, von Behr, to lay the matter before the King, and on the 13th received the answer that the King had decided that Saxony would raise no objection to Köchly's installation at Hamburg. However, the arrangement did not come off, as Köchly stayed on at the University of Zürich. It was not till 1864 that an invitation from the University of Heidelberg induced him to return to Germany.

III

WAGNER AND WEBER'S " SILVANA "

We know from Wagner's autobiography what reverence he had for Karl Maria von Weber ; from his boyhood he had been a Weber enthusiast, and in 1844 he had zealously advocated the transfer of Weber's mortal remains from St Mary's, Moorfields, in London, to Dresden, and had personally contributed much, by the funeral music and an oration by the grave in the Friedrichstadt Catholic Cemetery, to the solemnity of the occasion and the dignity of the ceremonial. In the face of this, it appears strange that the trusty chorus-master of the Dresden Court Theatre, Wilhelm Fischer, who wanted in 1855 to have Weber's *Silvana* produced, should state that Wagner expressed an unfavourable opinion on Weber's work. He writes to von Lüttichau, the General Manager :

DRESDEN
May 24, 1855

Will your Excellency permit me, without presuming to dictate to you, to propose Maria von Weber's *Silvana* for performance, and for that purpose to submit the libretto to careful consideration and revision?

When I made a similar proposal some years ago the Kapell-meisters Reissiger and Wagner refused to have a performance, as they were both of the opinion that it would not be to Maria von Weber's honour to produce one of his youthful works.

But in any case it would be interesting to all admirers of the immortal Weber to make the acquaintance of this work of his youth. The music has so much good stuff in it that the Master himself would have no cause to be ashamed of it; and the subject, in my opinion, with the dances, and especially the torch dance in the Finale, will give plenty of entertainment to ordinary people. . . .

WILHELM FISCHER, SENIOR

As, after Wagner's departure, Reissiger, one of the two who had opposed a former production of *Silvana*, held his post till 1859, it seems as if Fischer no longer had to fear any opposition on his part. Wagner thus appears to have been the chief cause of the previous refusal. Fischer, moreover, was a good friend of Wagner's, and would never have brought a false charge against him in his absence.

Thus we cannot doubt that this unfavourable opinion was really expressed, but it is equally certain that it was from no envy or jealousy on the part of Wagner; in spite of his roughness and his unconcealed dislike of certain tendencies in music, he was always willing and eager to give other great masters their due honour. He must, therefore, have been honestly convinced that *Silvana* was not likely to enhance the fame of the composer of *Preciosa* and *Euryanthe*, *Der Freischütz*, and *Oberon*, as it was a youthful work (it was written in 1810), a new version of *Das Waldmädchen*, which was Weber's earliest effort, composed in 1800 at the age of fourteen.

Fischer thought it best not to speak of this incident to his friend; at least, there is no reference to *Silvana* in Wagner's published letters of 1855 to Fischer. Von Lüttichau agreed, as his endorsement on the letter shows, to the performance, which accordingly took place on July 29, 1855, at the Court Theatre. The opera, however, has never found a permanent place in the *répertoire*, either at Dresden or elsewhere, and this seems to confirm Wagner's opinion of it.

IV

Botho von Hülsen on the Production of "Tannhäuser" in Berlin in 1856

Botho von Hülsen,[1] the General Manager of the Court Theatre at Berlin, was no great admirer of Wagner's art. His general attitude shows this beyond a doubt; and in numerous particular cases we see from the Master's letters to Liszt, Minna, and others how little he did for Wagner. What was done was impaired by inefficiency and by stinginess in money matters.

After Berlin had hesitated long over *Tannhäuser*, after Wagner's friends had for years been taking all imaginable trouble to get a good production of the opera, von Hülsen's ill-will and his partly open, partly covert opposition were overcome. According to the story in *Mein Leben*, Wagner was inclined to let matters go, feeling that his credit was sufficiently assured by the brilliant success of his works at other theatres. " Any failure that we may apprehend at Berlin could not damage the reputation of my work, though it might discredit the Berlin management," was his biting remark. From his account it was a " miserable performance," though the faithful Liszt, in his telegram of January 8, 1856, and his letter of the 14th, gives a rapturous description of it, making out that nearly everything, the singers, the orchestra, and the staging, was either excellent or at least meritorious, and only the chorus and the strings were faulty—an account which was evidently intended to put his morose friend in a better temper.

Thus it is interesting now to read Hülsen's own personal, undisguised expression of his views in a letter to the Dresden critic Dr Julius Pabst, written immediately after the first performance.

I thank you very much for your kindness in giving me news of the theatre. I was not surprised at the way in which the critics here have spoken of *Tannhäuser*. What more is there to be said ? It is clear that the piece excites party feeling ; some praise it above all measure, others loathe it. The fairest verdict is midway between the two. On one point all agree, in recognizing and praising the great care with which the work has been staged, not only from the musical, but from the scenic standpoint. The beauty and correctness of the costumes and the lifelike representation of the scenery were greatly admired. In the case of party feeling such as is manifest here the best, the only, course for the management to adopt is to rise above all parties, and that is what has been done here. But we must confess the truth ; our impartial opinion is that the work wearies both body and mind in the hearing. Consequently at the third performance we made cuts here and there, which improved the reception of the work and will be helpful in future. Besides, Wagner has provoked harsh criticism by his own book !

I know the drama of *Die Brüder*.[1] I should be glad if you would let me have it in the shape in which you got it. Mosenthal's latest piece requires lavish expense in the matter of scenery, as I realized when I read it. In other places, where less attention is paid to the scenic side than we give, and where *ballets* such as *Satanella* and *Ballanda* are unknown, any extraordinary splendour of scenery and costumes is far more of a draw to the general public than it is here. But here it is not so easy to make a success with these mere outside effects, and I generally object to them in a play.

You will soon hear from your wife how *Tannhäuser* goes, as she is coming to the opera to-morrow.

With my best respects,

HÜLSEN

BERLIN
January 18, 1856

V

REISSIGER'S LETTER TO RAFF ON THEATRICAL CONDITIONS AT DRESDEN AFTER THE REVOLUTION OF MAY 1849

Shortly before the revolution in May and the fire at the theatre Joachim Raff had sent the chief Kapellmeister Reissiger his work *König Alfred*, " a heroic grand opera in four acts, by Gotthold Logau, set to music by Joachim

Raff," which Reissiger sent back to him on May 16, 1849, with a letter giving a gloomy picture of theatrical conditions at Dresden. Following Reissiger's advice, Raff tried to get the piece done at Weimar, and Liszt's friendly influence succeeded in having it put on. Raff himself conducted the first performance, which, according to his account, was extremely successful, so that he ventured again to try Dresden. He explains the circumstances in his long covering letter to von Lüttichau, written from Weimar on July 21, 1851, with a request that the piece should be accepted for production. He adds :

> The libretto contains nothing that offends against the existing law of the Press. The music, midway between the extremes of grand opera as written by Rossini and Meyerbeer on the one hand, and the latest productions in Germany on the other, is more likely to satisfy differing tastes than to offend anyone's prejudice.

As an introduction, he encloses Reissiger's letter of May 16, 1849, which thus finds a place in the archives of the theatre.

DRESDEN
May 16, '49

MY DEAR FRIEND,

I could not acknowledge the receipt of your score till to-day ; we are stunned and crushed to the earth by the terrible times we have just been through. Dresden is ruined, and we artists are ruined with it. Our great Opera House, in which our splendid scenery and costumes were stored, is in ruins. Yesterday all the singers and actors had their notices. We do not know yet what the King will do ; but it is certain that we shall have to begin again on a very small scale. Owing to the disaster to Dresden and the political excitement, the King cannot yet think of amusements. The next new operas down for performance were Halévy's *Val d'Andorre* and Meyerbeer's *Prophète*. When shall we be able to give them ? Your opera's chances are quite hopeless for a long time to come. It is of no use to show anything to the management now—they are helpless; so you had better look after your score yourself (though it is quite safe with me), if you do not wish to lose a whole year over it. Write to Berlin, or write to Liszt at Weimar, where he is very influential, and has taken a great deal of trouble over Wagner's *Tannhäuser*. Their resources there, especially the singers, are excellent. Councillor Winkler, to whom I showed part of your letter, joins me in regretting the fatal disaster that has destroyed your prospects for a long time. We would gladly have done our best for you ; your overture is excellent—finely and effectively scored. Give me your sympathy, and hope with me for better times to come for our art.

With sincere regards,
Yours,
C. G. REISSIGER

With reference to this matter, we may give the following details. The notice dismissing the actors was put up by the General Management on May 11, 1849, to take effect on August 31, 1849 ; but, only two days after Reissiger wrote his despairing letter to Raff, the joyful news came that King Frederick Augustus had provided for carrying on the Court Theatre.

Reissiger recommended the opera for production, in 1851, in the following very favourable criticism :

> This opera, the work of a gifted and enterprising musician, who is only too anxious to be always clear and natural, possesses great merit. The music is effective, mostly fresh, and, in spite of considerable difficulties for the singers, who will have to struggle with many unusual modulations and startling intervals, is well worth the trouble of performance. The scoring, though often rather thick, shows great assiduity ; it is well chosen, full of charm, and most effective. As we can cast this opera well, I think I may strongly recommend it to the Management. The choruses are difficult, but fine and effective.

Apparently, however, Reissiger's recommendation was in vain ; at least, Raff's *König Alfred* is not mentioned under 1851 or any later year in the list of original productions and rehearsals of new operas given by Prölss in his theatrical history.

NOTES *

Page 17, *note* 1. Wagner had got up a similar enthusiastic demonstration in honour of Frederick Augustus II in 1844, when it was proposed to offer the King an improvised poetical and musical welcome on his return from England. Wagner described this many years after, with obvious satisfaction, in *Mein Leben.*

Page 17, *note* 2. Printed in Wagner's collected works under the title, " Wie verhalten sich republikanische Bestrebungen dem Königthume gegenüber ? " † Wagner defends himself rather cleverly against the charges incurred with regard to this speech in a letter to von Lüttichau of June 18, 1848, which Houston Stewart Chamberlain (in *Richard Wagner*) has given in facsimile. While in 1848 Wagner makes the King say, " I declare Saxony to be a Free State," two years later, on June 26, 1850, he maintains the exact opposite. In a letter of that date to Frau Julie Ritter he adopts the standpoint that drastic reforms can only be carried out by force, and not by any treaty or agreement with those who do not agree with them. He closes with the sceptical question, " *Can* a prince decree a republic ? " But was not that just what he wanted on June 14, 1848 ?

Page 18, *note* 1. Bakunin used harsh expressions about Wagner at his examination in the Königstein (September 19, 1849). " I soon saw that Wagner was a mere dreamer, and although I talked to him, even on politics, I never worked in common with him."

Page 20, *note* 1. We may mention here the latest account, which sums up previous works on the subject—Georg Müller's *Richard Wagner in der Mai-Revolution,* 1849 (Dresden, 1919).

Page 21, *note* 1. The *dossier,* compiled in 1856, bears the title, " Evidence against the former Kapellmeister Richard Wagner, as to his share in the revolt here in May 1849."

Page 22, *note* 1. The Wagner *dossier* reports concerning these meetings that F. W. Hering, the gardener who leased the Menagerie Garten at Friedrichstadt, declared that in the cottage in the garden, away from the street, which had been let to the Naumann family since the end of the winter (that is, for the last six weeks), numerous secret meetings took place, at first once a week, but, shortly before the May revolt, daily. Twenty or thirty men used to come, some on foot, some in droshkies, usually at 3 P.M., and stay till evening, perhaps till nightfall. He said he recognized " none of these persons except Kapellmeister Wagner, who is personally known to me." On these occasions the

---

* Page references to German works have usually been omitted in these Notes, as likely to be of little use to readers of the translation.

† " The Relations between Republican Aspirations and the Monarchy."

blinds were drawn, even by daylight. These statements, in so far as they involved the Naumann family, were flatly and successfully contradicted, so that Hering withdrew many of his statements, and only persisted in saying that some men, Wagner among them, used to meet in the rooms of a certain Dr Schwartz, a tenant of Naumann's. This Dr Schwartz was none other than Bakunin.

Page 22, *note* 2. As to this, see the passage from Röckel's evidence given in the Wagner *dossier* :

"Wagner, who was interested in arming the people, had lent me his garden for a discussion on this project with Professor Schubert and First Lieutenant Schreiber; the latter, who was kept away by his military duties, wrote to Wagner, excusing himself for not having come. As in this letter there were some notes that were really meant for me, to help on my work in arming the people, Wagner sent it to me."

This Schreiber addressed to Wagner, but it was found among Röckel's papers. Later on another meeting took place in Wagner's garden, at which, besides Schreiber, Lieutenants Müller and von Erdmannsdorf, Professor Semper and Dr Munde, Röckel and Wagner were present. Schreiber was called in especially to discuss the question of the volunteer artillery.

Page 22, *note* 3. The brassfounder Karl Wilhelm Oehme, in his very precise statement, which he firmly maintained, denounced Röckel and Wagner as the two who ordered the hand-grenades, while Röckel denied that he was concerned in it and said that Wagner alone ordered them, which Oehme contradicted.

Page 23, *note* 1. Wagner's activity on the Kreuzturm (observing the positions of the troops and the approach of the insurgents from the country) was attested by several witnesses, especially his share in sending messages, throwing down notes tied to stones from the tower gallery ; while Wagner, in describing his meeting with Röckel in the Plauen Vorstadt (or Seevorstadt), says that Röckel led the troop of young gymnasts who met them there to the Altmarkt. Röckel, in his examination of July 30, 1849, says that the Zittau troop went with Wagner.

Page 23, *note* 2. As to this temporary absence from Dresden, Wagner himself informs us that on the morning of May 8 he went with Minna to his father-in-law, Wolfram, at Chemnitz, but came back to Dresden on the morning of the 9th, to leave the city, however, on the same day. On the way, at Oederan and Freiberg, Wagner, according to the testimony of eye-witnesses, met the lagging and reluctant troop of the Chemnitz town guard, which was urged to quicken its march on Dresden by messengers from the Provisional Government, "among whom appeared Kapellmeister Wagner." Wagner's own words, in his letter of May 15, 1851, to Eduard Röckel, confirm this charge.

Page 23, *note* 3. To this summary the Minister of Justice, von Behr, added later the following note :

"According to a verbal communication of the Minister von Zeschau, Wagner still owes 5000 thalers to the privy purse. Wagner's wife, on being questioned, gave assurance that a release had been given from this debt, which Councillor von Lüttichau would confirm. v. B."

Page 24, *note* 1. He did not write to the King himself (as a report, which he contradicted in a letter of February 8, 1850, to Uhlig, made out), but to Frau von Lüttichau, whom he respected and trusted more than he did her husband, his former chief. He asked her to take the proper steps toward approaching the King. Wagner himself only mentions, in his autobiography, a letter to Röckel and Bakunin, which he forwarded to them by the mediation of Frau von Lüttichau.

Page 26, *note* 1. This made a specially bad impression in Saxony. Prince John, brother of King Frederick Augustus, wrote from the Königstein on May 28, 1849, to his son Albert, on active service in Schleswig :

" The shamelessness of some of these rebels is remarkable. Kapellmeister Wagner conducted an operatic rehearsal at Weimar, and called upon the Minister, Watzdorf, and even upon the Grand Duchess— and an hour after arrived the warrant for his arrest."

In this correspondence Wagner is not mentioned again, except briefly on May 20, among those against whom warrants were out.

Page 28, *note* 1. Wolf Adolf August von Lüttichau, born at Ulbersdorf February 16, 1786. First a forest superintendent, appointed General Manager on September 4, 1824, and later Privy Councillor. He retired on April 1, 1862, and died at Dresden February 16, 1863. His wife was Ida von Knobelsdorf (born 1798, married 1818, died 1856). As a contrast to Wagner's many hard words about Lüttichau see his remarks in *Mein Leben*.

Page 28, *note* 2. He wrote to his brother-in-law Hermann Brockhaus on February 2, 1851 : " My position at Dresden had long been irksome to me, and, apart from political troubles, I should have had to give it up sooner or later, if I wished to preserve my integrity as man and artist." He was only sorry that he had not been able to retire from his subordinate position before.

Page 28, *note* 3. Later on, too, he always loudly complains when he has had to rehearse and conduct operas or concerts.

Page 30, *note* 1. " Devil take it, we shan't starve ! " he writes in a letter to Heine.

Page 31, *note* 1. Carl Schurz, *Denkwürdigkeiten* (Berlin, 1906) :

" The most noteworthy acquaintance I made at that time (autumn of 1849) was Richard Wagner, who, in consequence of his share in the revolution at Dresden, was also living at Zürich as a refugee He had already composed some of his chief works, but his greatness was realized only among a small circle. He was not liked by those who shared his fate at the time. He was thought an extremely bumptious and arrogant fellow, with whom nobody could get on, and who behaved very badly to his wife, a pretty, good-natured, but not remarkably intelligent woman. If anyone had foretold his future splendid career the prophet would have found small credit among us."

Page 31, *note* 2. Letter to Minna August 11, 1849, and letter to Clara Wolfram December 1, 1849, in which Wagner mentions that for Minna's sake he had tried to get the expression " as a common criminal " withdrawn from the warrant for his arrest. In the warrant of May 16, 1849, there is nothing about " a common criminal." The words are, " in connexion with the recent disturbances, in which he is known to have taken an active part," a phrase which he could hardly dispute. In the second warrant (June 11, 1853) it runs, " on account of his share in the Dresden rising in 1849."

Page 32, note 1. The source for the following statement is a small file of papers, in the archives of the Ministry of the Interior, comprising various police reports and so on concerning " the former Kapell-meister R. W. from Dresden."

Page 32, note 2. These Austrian connexions may be referred either to his associating with Liberals during his visit to Vienna in July 1848 or to the fact that he was in close association with Röckel, who had gone to Prague on revolutionary business shortly before the outbreak of the revolution of May. Wagner had sent Röckel at Prague the portentous and well-known letter which plays a considerable part in the criminal prosecutions of 1849. People in Austria were well informed on the subject, since two Austrian officials were present (officially) at the examinations of Röckel in July, August, and September 1849.

Page 33, note 1. Wagner mentions Heimberger, the young Galician, in his autobiography. He was introduced to him by Bakunin, with a view to Heimberger's having violin lessons from the Dresden musician Lipinski.

Page 33, note 2. Eberhardt gave the desired information to the Prague police magistrate Wermann on February 13, but added that so far nothing was known of any connexion between Wagner and the leaders of the Swiss revolutionary party, especially Heimberger.

Page 34, note 1. Other celebrated persons were not protected from the suspicion of the police by their musical eminence. When in October 1851 Wilhelmina Schröder-Devrient passed through Dresden with her husband, von Bock, a Livonian, she was summoned by the police to answer for the inflammatory speech she had delivered to the people on May 3, 1849, from a window of the " Lion " Pharmacy, as the body of a man shot at the Arsenal was carried to the Altmarkt. Further proceedings on this serious charge were graciously quashed by the King, but the lady had to pay the costs.

Page 34, note 2. Wagner's letter to Uhlig November 11, 1851. He also told Minna the story about the amnesty on November 9.

Page 36, note 1. He assures Uhlig on October 12 and 14, 1852, " I cannot see how else it could be, for nothing would induce me to apply for an amnesty myself." However, a trip to Vienna or Berlin to hear his opera would do him good. He will not hear of Saxony : " I am no longer a Saxon."

Page 38, note 1. As Hereditary Grand Duke he had, just after Wagner's flight, accepted his dedication of *Tannhäuser*. See Wagner's fine letter to him August 7, 1849.

Page 40, note 1. In his book *Aus dem Leben der Königin Carola von Sachsen* von Schimpff declares the rumours about Napoleon formerly suing for Carola's hand to be unfounded ; but the fact that this question for some time occupied the minds of those most concerned is proved by Prince John George's biography of King Albert of Saxony.

Page 44, *note* 1. However, Liszt visited Zürich in July, and Wagner spent a delightful week with him, of which he speaks enthusiastically in his autobiography. But neither Liszt nor Wagner's niece, Johanna Wagner, went with him to St Moritz. His travelling companion was Georg Herwegh, the poet, with whom he went on July 14, *via* Coire, to St Moritz, where he stayed till August.

Page 44, *note* 2. This is scarcely the right view of the case. Wagner's letter to Breitkopf and Härtel June 28, 1853, describing the warrant as " the last new incivility of the Dresden police," expresses not pride, but annoyance. So, too, the words of his letter to Fischer July 1, 1853, " I am glad that the Saxon police have made it impossible for me to see my operas performed—it would only annoy me," betray rather bitterness of feeling than a self-satisfied vanity. He also writes quite jestingly about it to his step-sister, Cecilia Avenarius ; the police, he says, have been taken in by one of their own spies, and, for his part, he has no intention of crossing the German frontier.

Page 44, *note* 3. That Wagner had such fits of generosity we know from his own letters. On February 11, 1853, he wrote to Liszt that he had had a few copies of the *Nibelung* poem printed at his own expense, three of them, splendidly bound, for the Grand Duchess of Weimar, Princess Augusta of Prussia, and Liszt himself. Only fifty copies were printed.

Page 45, *note* 1. Compare Liszt's letters of July 17 and 25, 1853. This is Wagner's letter of July 14, 1853, to Charles Alexander, in which he thanks him warmly for his kindness, and especially for the faculty of comprehension that allows him to honour an artist, in spite of his having a bad name as a politician.

Page 45, *note* 2. Letters to Liszt August 25, September 19 and 23, 1853. The French Minister at Berne was then the Comte Alfred de Salignac-Fénélon.

Page 46, *note* 1. As to Schurz, who was concerned in the Baden rising, see note on p. 193. Wagner's relations with the Wesendonk family might also appear suspicious, since a member of the family was under police observation as a " strong democrat," as we see from the following report :

" Haan (a commercial traveller from Coblenz) was, during the troublous times of 1848 and 1849, intimately acquainted with several leading democrats, Raveaux at Cologne and Wesendonk at Düsseldorf ; the former is now dead, the latter no longer in Germany."

Otto Wesendonk lived at Düsseldorf 1848–50, in 1850 went to America, and in 1851 to Switzerland.

Page 46, *note* 2. Letter to Uhlig March 25, 1852. Compare the police reports of 1858 :

" Kinkel associates only with Mazzini and Ledru-Rollin ; their meeting-place is the house of the Socialist Fräulein Meysenburg [*sic*]. She has been employed by Mazzini as his agent, through whose hands his letters pass ; you have to apply to her in order to see Mazzini."

And, further :

" The above-mentioned ' Fräulein Meysenburg ' is, of course, the well-known Malvida von Meysenbug, of whom we know by other

reports that she lives near London, is in close communication with
political refugees, and is engaged in translating Herzen's writings and
other revolutionary works."

Page 46, *note* 3. Compare the Dresden police report August 5, 1853 :
" Eduard Rémenyi, a violinist, born at Erlau, in Hungary, 22 years
old. When very young he was a dispatch-rider for Generals Klapka
and Görgey ; he went to America with his brother, took out naturaliza-
tion papers at New York, March 15, 1850, and toward the end of 1850
returned to the Continent."

A later report, of September 24, 1853, says :
" The violinist Eduard Rémenyi, . . . though ostensibly associating
only with musicians and lovers of music, has been in communication
with the well-known democrat I. Dresel at Geisenheim, whom he often
visited there. According to his own account, he now lives at Weimar
with Kapellmeister Liszt ; he is an intimate friend of Richard Wagner,
and has lately paid a visit to him in Switzerland."

The description of this once well-known musician is given in the
Dresden confidential police report of May 6, 1854 :
" According to trustworthy information, the violinist who calls
himself Eduard Rémenyi is in fact a Hungarian refugee, but his real
name is Hoffmann. He is the son of Heinrich Hoffmann, a journey-
man goldsmith, living at Pesth, and is at present travelling through the
German states as a go-between for the members of the revolutionary
party, of which he is an active member. As he is merely provided
with a passport of September 25, 1852, from the American Embassy
at Paris, and this passport was granted on his bare declaration that he
wished to become an American citizen, the Saxon police authorities
have given orders to arrest the said Hoffmann if he should enter Saxony,
to submit his personal effects to a close examination, to examine the
prisoner as to his personal circumstances, the purpose of his journey,
and his connexions with others, and to take any further steps in consequence of the results of this inquiry. It is reported that Hoffmann
gave a violin recital at Wiesbaden in March of this year, under the
name of Rémenyi."

Even in 1860 Rémenyi appeared a suspicious person, as we see from
a Berlin weekly police report of April 23, 1860.

Page 47, *note* 1. Dr Franz Dingelstedt (he was ennobled later) after his work
as a dramatic critic at Stuttgart became manager of the Court Theatre
at Munich 1851–56, and was a personal friend of King Maximilian II.

Page 48, *note* 1. As a matter of fact, no rehearsals of *Tannhäuser* took place
at Munich in 1854 ; it was not till 1855 that Dingelstedt was able to
produce it.

Page 50, *note* 1. How inaccurate this statement is is proved by many passages
in *Mein Leben* and the letters to Minna. The receipts often fell below
expectations, and still more often were very unpunctual and came only
after continual reminders, direct and indirect. However, there *were*
receipts, which contributed to maintain Wagner's household.

Page 50, *note* 2. We need not state that this mean and stupid accusation is
quite unfounded ; there is not even a trace of any such charge in the

papers relating to Wagner's revolutionary activity. As to the charge of setting fire to the palace, which is apparently alluded to, see pp. 171-172 of the present work.

Page 50, *note* 3. The reference is to Wagner's controversial writings on art, *Die Kunst und die Revolution* (1849), *Das Kunstwerk der Zukunft* (1850), *Das Judenthum in der Musik* (1850), *Oper und Drama* (1851).

Page 51, *note* 1. The letter bears no date, but belongs to the early part of October.

Page 52, *note* 1. His fine human qualities, his unselfishness and philanthropy, were gratefully recognized even by those who opposed his political doctrines. Even Heinrich von Treitschke, in *Die Zukunft der deutschen Mittelstaaten* (1866), calls him " the most amiable of the house of Wettin."

Page 54, *note* 1. Ferdinand Zschinsky, later ennobled as von Zschinsky, President of the Council and Minister of Justice from May 2, 1849, to his death on October 28, 1858.

Page 56, *note* 1. Prince Albert, brother of Ernest II, the Liberal Duke of Coburg-Gotha, was so free from prejudice as to meet another Dresden revolutionist, Gottfried Semper, on friendly terms.

Page 58, *note* 1. It was also false information that caused the report from Dresden that Wagner " is going to America with his sister Johanna " to be circulated as news from London. It is well known that Wagner had no sister of that name : Johanna, the singer, was his niece.

Page 62, *note* 1. There is no justification for Glasenapp's attack on Gottfried Keller and the gossiping Zürich papers, which put about the report that the Master had already sent a petition for pardon to the King of Saxony, and that Semper and Köchly had suddenly shown a desire for amnesty. But while Semper and Köchly protested against such a supposition, Wagner, according to Keller, was in such a position that he had to be silent about the story, in order not to spoil his chances. " He [Keller] fails to give any evidence as to what possible consideration could have prevented the Master from correcting the false report if he wanted to." Glasenapp ought to have been more cautious, and not to have tried to know more than Keller or Wagner himself ; for, in fact, Wagner knew very well why he did not contradict the report. As an honourable man he could only be silent, for the portentous petition that so excites Glasenapp had really been sent and could not be denied. The fairly definite allusions in the correspondence with Liszt show that something was going on about an amnesty.

Page 64, *note* 1. Wagner more than once protested against the charge of ingratitude toward King Frederick Augustus, which he felt bitterly. He declared that he gave full return for all he got. The charge of exciting the members of the orchestra against the Government is certainly exaggerated ; it rests chiefly on a speech that Wagner made on February 12, 1849, at a meeting of the orchestra. Von Lüttichau questioned Wagner on February 14, reproaching him with his speech ; and he refused to accept Wagner's explanation. We may consult the minutes of this interview, taken by the secretary to the management, Karl Theodor Winkler. They are quoted by Robert Prölss in his history of the Court Theatre at Dresden. Chamberlain, in his *Richard Wagner*, justly points out that many passages in this minute (Wagner's expressions and notes by the reporter) show that both parties, Wagner and the management, were considering his resigning his post before the outbreak of the revolution, and von Lüttichau undertook to refer the matter to the decision of the King. This, as he says, puts another face on the charge of " ingratitude."

Page 69, *note* 1. Moritz Christian Hänel, Privy Councillor, Chief Councillor of the Ministry of Justice.

Page 69, *note* 2. This document, which has been used by Dinger and Müller, need not be discussed further, since Wagner's revolutionary activities will not be related again.

Page 82, *note* 1. The letter may have been already sent for incorporation in the biography of King Albert, in which it is printed ; but as it is there quite unconnected with Wagner's whole career, and has consequently hardly become known in musical literature, it seems not only desirable, but necessary to reproduce it here in full from the original.

Page 89, *note* 1. The principle that proceedings could not be dropped so long as the accused evaded trial by flight was not peculiar to Saxony, or to King John, but was held elsewhere. For instance, when Joseph Görres was invited to Munich, and consequently, on September 5, 1826, asked King Frederick William III of Prussia to annul the proceedings against him in Prussia, the King decided, on October 3, that as Görres had eluded trial by flight seven years before and lived abroad during that time, it was not proper to cancel the proceedings and allow him to return to Germany.

Page 92, *note* 1. The Austrian envoy at Berne was Baron Ferdinand von Mensshengen, appointed in 1856.

Page 93, *note* 1. According to the official notice to the police, he arrived on the 30th. The discrepancy is explained by the fact that his taking rooms at the Palazzo Giustiniani on the 30th was notified to the police, but his arrival at the Hotel Danieli on the 29th was not. There are several palaces of the former name on the Grand Canal. Wagner's account in his autobiography, his letter to Minna of October 28, and the official description, " by St Barnabas," in the Austrian police papers show that the Palazzo Giustiniani next to the Palazzo Foscari is the building that is meant.

Page 93, *note* 2. Karl Ferdinand, Count von Buol-Schauenstein. Born May 17, 1797, Austrian Ambassador at various German and foreign Courts, Privy Councillor in 1844, Minister of Foreign Affairs 1852–59, died October 28, 1865.

Page 93, *note* 3. Johann Franz, Baron Kempen von Fichtenstamm (born June 26, 1793), a distinguished officer of high merit who was also engaged in the study of war history. In 1849 he was appointed Inspector-General of the Gendarmerie, and in 1852 Chief of Police. He was a Privy Councillor in 1851, in 1854 was made a baron, retired in 1859, and died November 29, 1863.

Page 95, *note* 1. Hugo, Count von Traun-Abensberg, born September 20, 1828. At first *attaché* and councillor of embassy at various Courts,

then Secretary of Legation at the Court of Dresden, later on Master
of Ceremonies and Master of the Hunt.   The Ambassador, after 1856,
was Prince Richard von Metternich-Winneburg (son of the Chancellor),
who was born January 7, 1829, and died March 1, 1895.

Page 96, *note* 1. The chief Councillor of the Venice police was Dr Angelo
Crespi.

Page 97, *note* 1. The Chief of Police at Venice was Cavaliere Giuseppe
Franceschinis de Fidalma.

Page 99, *note* 1. Wagner speaks in a letter to Minna (October 28, 1858) of
a Count Kalenberg, whom he twice had to refuse to see.   The
Gallenbergs were a family of Carniola.

Page 99, *note* 2. Count Cajetan Alexander von Bissingen-Nippenburg. Born
March 18, 1806, Privy Councillor, Austrian Governor of Venice, died
May 10, 1890.

Page 100, *note* 1. The Grand Duke of Baden, as Wagner wrote to Minna
(September 14, 1858), was to obtain the Saxon authorization for Wagner
to come to Germany for the production of a new opera, whenever he
desired.   Possibly, as he thought, a complete amnesty would be granted
by next Easter, as the Saxon Government was busy with a plan for
allowing the refugees to enter Germany, except Saxony.   He was no
longer thinking of Saxony, but would prefer Baden for a long stay.

Page 101, *note* 1. Though he constantly declares that he must hear his operas,
to keep up his artistic and creative faculty, he writes on December 5,
1858, to Liszt :
    " Whether, for instance, I produce my *Nibelungen* or not is essentially
a matter of indifference to me ; I shall still complete it, since my in-
spiration and power in such work does not rest on hopes which I cannot
realize without the help of particular persons."

Page 103, *note* 1. This has a different tone from the letter of September 14
(see note, p. 100), even when we consider that the latter deliberately
intended to meet Minna's views and wishes.   On September 27, 1858,
he wrote to Tichatschek about his wife's journey to Dresden :
    " I myself should be glad to settle in Dresden—in a private capacity,
of course.   One does need a home, and I have nothing against Dresden
—anywhere else I should feel a stranger.   Heaven grant that your
august King may at last show mercy, put an end to my unfortunate
condition, the penalty for having been once carried away by the general
madness.   Let us hope for this ! "
    Here, too, he wanted to produce a favourable impression on his
correspondent.   This temper did not last long ; a change soon came.
On November 14, 1858, he says, " Good God ! What good is Dresden,
in any case ? " and, in the second letter of that date, " It is frightful for
you to have to go to the police yourself !   The devil !   Is there nobody
there to take these troubles off your hands ?   That's where I realize
the meanness of Dresden."

Page 104, *note* 1. This interesting letter was first deposited by von Lüttichau
in the archives of the General Management (there is now a separate
portfolio relating to Richard Wagner), and then given to the dramatist
Dr Julius Pabst, who, as secretary of the management, was von Lüttichau's

right-hand man. A copy by a clerk, endorsed by Pabst, was substituted for it in the archives. The original letter was religiously preserved in Pabst's family ; it passed, on the marriage of his daughter, to her husband, the Consul-General Fritz Chrambach, who kindly placed it at my disposal. This most interesting document was printed by Glasenapp in the collection of Wagner's letters to Lüttichau published in an illustrated fortnightly magazine, *Die Musik*, but inaccurately and omitting some important passages. I print the letter from the original in Wagner's handwriting.

Page 104, *note* 2. This assertion is not true, as is shown by the foregoing narrative ; and Wagner himself proves it, for on April 3, 1862, he writes to Minna, " I have always duly received the negative answers."

Page 110, *note* 1. Von Lüttichau drafted out this answer on the top of the first page of Wagner's letter.

Page 112, *note* 1. Franceschinis sent direct to Kempen, at Vienna, a copy of the report he furnished to von Bissingen.

Page 117, *note* 1. Zschinsky (and with him Rabenhorst, the Minister of War) was raised to the hereditary nobility expressly on account of services in suppressing the revolution, and the fact showed King John's own political views. In John's draft of the letter to Zschinsky of May 3, 1856, he says : " How could I forget those men who stood so firmly by him [his brother, Frederick Augustus II] ? Indeed, how could I fail to remember you who in that fateful hour entered the King's Council and assumed the responsibility of the grave measures that had to be taken ? " Von Behr's appointment as Minister of Justice was suggested to him by the King on November 19, as he himself says in his letter to King John on November 20, in which he complies with the King's wish, though with some misgivings.

Page 117, *note* 2. Though he goes on to say, on February 27, " I have no hope, and am quite resigned. I don't want their amnesty any more, and should not know what to do with it ! " On March 1 he speaks in a different tone. " I believe I shall get my amnesty through it [the letter to von Behr] just because it is now of no consequence to me."

Page 117, *note* 3. This document was printed in *Die Musik*, not, however, from the original, but from the rough draft, with its many omissions and discrepancies, so that it is necessary to reprint it in its final form. Altmann says it was addressed to von Beust, although the real facts of the case are clear from the letters to Minna, confirmed by the papers of the Ministry. The letter was printed in the *Dresdener Anzeiger* of July 23, 1902, with the wrong address and other mistakes, and with a foolish note, suggesting that King John was incensed against Wagner by von Beust. Our narrative shows that there was no need for such a supposition, as John always disliked Wagner.

Page 122, *note* 1. On February 1 he had written to Karl Klindworth, " If the two Princes of the Confederation who are friendly to me do not exert pressure the Saxon will not pardon me." He had spoken to Minna on January 25, even more confidently about the help he expected from the Diet.

Page 123, *note* 1. On April 2, 1859, Kempen informed Count von Buol, the

Minister, that "the well-known political refugee" (as the police always regarded Wagner) Richard Wagner had left Venice on March 25 and gone to Lucerne. Von Buol passed on the news to the Austrian Ambassador at Dresden, Prince Metternich.

Page 125, *note* 1. Letter to Minna September 6, 1859. Wagner speaks here of a "Privy Councillor Behr," who would see to the petition. The name cannot be right, for there was no Privy Councillor Behr in Dresden at the time, and it cannot be von Behr, the Minister of Justice. Plainly it is the Clerk of the Closet to the King, Privy Councillor Wilhelm Immanuel Bär, who is meant, for petitions addressed direct to the King came through the Cabinet office.

Page 126, *note* 1. His forlorn position, when he thought himself forgotten by all, is shown also by his letters to Hans von Bülow in December 1859.

Page 130, *note* 1. Albin Leo von Seebach, born January 31, 1811, at Langensalza. Baron in 1855, Count in 1864, Ambassador Extraordinary and Minister Plenipotentiary for Saxony at Paris and Brussels, died June 16, 1884. It may be mentioned here as a curious fact that von Seebach himself was for a time politically suspect at Paris, and was kept under observation by the French Government, not from fear of revolution, but for reasons of foreign policy, as France was then engaged in the Crimean War. Report (to Dresden) from London, May 14, 1855 :

"I heard lately from good sources that the French Government keeps the Saxon Embassy and Herr von Seebach under special observation. It is known that Baron Seebach is in touch with the Russian Embassy at Brussels, and forwards reports from Russian agents at Paris. Young Decazes, son of the Duke, who often visits the Saxon Embassy, is suspected of being a Russian agent, and so is a certain Herr von Wolfers."

Page 130, *note* 2. Wagner passes lightly over more recent events and the course of the negotiations, especially his own repeated petitions and letters.

Page 135, *note* 1. Even the mulatto actor Ira Aldridge, in whose Othello Wagner took an interest merely as a dramatic artist, appears in the weekly police reports (April and December 1858) as politically objectionable. One of the Saxon rebels of May 1859 was the former theologian Gerber, who afterward lived as a refugee in London. Wagner in 1857 speaks of him as a friend whom he is glad to see. He also associated with Hermann Köchly, but the acquaintance never became a friendship.

Page 136, *note* 1. The Grand Duke Charles Alexander of Weimar expressed this point of view very clearly in a letter he wrote toward the end of 1860, at Liszt's suggestion :

"It is my function, as Grand Duke of Weimar, to recognize all real merit in science, art, and industry. Wagner deserves my fullest recognition, for in the world of music he is unique. His operas, so eminently German in character, have for years found a home on the Weimar stage, a fact which we are proud to acknowledge. He is now about to produce *Tannhäuser* in Paris, and no doubt will be rewarded by the Emperor, who has invited him to produce the opera in his capital.

I should not like it to be said that a great German composer has no honour in Germany, nor do I care to have him wait for a German order till after he has received a French one."

The fact that the Grand Duke's sense of what was fitting was prevented from expressing itself in action by ministerial objections does not diminish the credit due to this highminded prince.

Page 136, *note* 2. Wagner was informed of Augusta's action by von Seebach, who asked him later on to thank the Princess personally, and explained that this proof of his gratitude would please the King of Saxony.

Page 140, *note* 1. We can find no trace of the sources of these reports. The " confidential police information " and " weekly reports," often quoted in early chapters of this book, have nothing bearing on this point. Richard Wagner's name does not appear in the files for the years 1859–61. Possibly the reference is merely to verbal reports, as von Seebach, at Dresden, could only hear these personally from von Beust.

Page 140, *note* 2. Leo von Zychlinsky was deeply involved in the revolution. As Adjutant of the third (Neustadt) battalion of the town guard, he had taken part in many revolutionary acts, stirring up the town guard to fight, and, it was supposed, spreading the order to set the Opera House on fire.

Page 141, *note* 1. Even Heubner, who was especially guilty as a member of the Provisional Government, was pardoned.

Page 143, *note* 1. In von Beust's draft the original words were, " Let Wagner enter without further question " ; but this has been struck out.

Page 143, *note* 2. In von Beust's original draft the following passage occurs :

" His Majesty's intentions are to be carried out in the following manner : as and when Wagner has occasion for so doing, he shall give notice thereof either through your Excellency or directly to the Ministry of Foreign Affairs here, whereupon the necessary information shall be sent to the Government concerned, in order that Wagner may safely take his journey to the particular place."

But this version was not approved by King John, who wrote under it with his own hand :

" I prefer that Wagner should apply to the Government of the country where he wants to go, and the necessary steps will be taken at *their* request. If you agree with this I beg you to send me the draft as altered."

Von Beust's first version was struck out, and the passage drafted in the sense just stated.

Page 144, *note* 1. Wagner's expression " a few days ago " can only be explained by supposing that, before the official written declaration of the answer to his petition was received, he had had private and confidential information of the arrival of the dispatch from Dresden on the 20th, or else that the report of the decision taken at Dresden on July 15 had come to the knowledge of his friends in Germany, waiting in anxious suspense, before the Ministerial letter reached Paris on its rather slow official journey. Otherwise there must be a mistake in the date, July 22, in the letter to Mathilde.

Page 150, *note* 1. As there were difficulties in the way of getting a Saxon passport, Pourtalès, ever helpful, provided a Prussian passport for the journey to Germany.

Page 151, *note* 1. Just after the *Tannhäuser* scandal at Paris Liszt wrote to Charles Alexander, on March 17, 1861, repeating the request he had made three months before (that is, at the end of 1860) " to bestow on my noble and illustrious friend R. Wagner the Cross [of the Order of the Falcon]." Later on in the year the Grand Duke resolved to grant the request, and sent Liszt the order for Wagner, with a short (undated) note :

" Here is the bird, dear friend and Master ! I sent it you because I think you will enjoy giving it to the composer of the *Nibelungen*. Please give it to him yourself from me, and tell him that I asked you to do this in order to make the gift more valuable, and as a proof of the esteem I have for him."

An opportunity came early in August 1861, when Wagner visited Liszt for the Weimar Musical Festival ; but opposing influences must again have succeeded in preventing Liszt from handing the order to Wagner.

Page 151, *note* 2. On July 12, 1861, he had written to Mathilde Wesendonk that he wanted Minna to settle in Dresden. " For my part I do not intend to settle anywhere. It is not my fate to woo the Muse among the comforts of home. . . . I must devote the rest of my life to wandering." So too, on July 14, he writes to Peter Cornelius, " I shall be a wanderer for the rest of my life."

Page 153, *note* 1. *Sachsens Erhebung und das Zuchthaus zu Waldheim*, by August Röckel.

Page 153, *note* 2. Louisabeth was later a member of the Court Theatre company at Vienna.

Page 154, *note* 1. The order to release Röckel from prison, with a command to leave Saxony within twenty-four hours—it was not an amnesty—followed on January 4, 1862. Early on January 10 he left for Weimar.

Page 155, *note* 1. Letter to Minna January 10, 1862 : " Look up Seebach and remind him."

Page 157, *note* 1. The reference is to the letter of July 26, 1860 (see pp. 143–144), which von Seebach forwarded to Dresden July 29, 1860. Wagner did not write any letter to King John in 1861.

Page 159, *note* 1. Certificate in his own handwriting, with a small black seal and with the monogram A.P. The important evidence is given verbatim, but the purely medical details of the condition of the various organs and of the symptoms of disease are, of course, omitted.

Page 159, *note* 2. Here Pusinelli makes a mistake in the dates. Minna stayed at Schandau till the beginning of October 1859 and in Dresden till November. In a long letter of October 3, 1859, Wagner explained to his friend Anton Pusinelli why it was necessary for Minna to move to Paris. In Dresden his wife would be " always in an environment that could only have bad effects on her. It was most fortunate for my wife that she had you as her doctor, but it was unfortunate that it had to be in Dresden." Pusinelli died March 31, 1878.

Page 161, *note* 1. From the original draft, initialled by King John, von Behr,

Hänel, and Krug. On the same page, just below, is the draft of the orders to the Dresden District Court, also initialled by King John, von Behr, and the Councillors of the Ministry, but dated March 27.

Page 162, *note* 1. Jenny Ney (after her marriage Bürde-Ney) had been a member of the opera company at Dresden since 1853, and was very popular.

Page 162, *note* 2. It is questionable whether he would have had much success, in spite of Augusta's support, considering Hülsen's cold, even hostile, attitude. Wagner himself relates that Hülsen successfully opposed a performance of *Tannhäuser* which Pourtalès tried to arrange at Berlin for the composer's benefit.

Page 162, *note* 3. Wagner had in his petition mentioned the state of Minna's health as well as the interests of his art; but he forgets that for years he had been much disturbed at not obtaining an amnesty, and for two years had rested all his hopes on securing this by von Seebach's help. He seems to forget too that during the last weeks he had constantly been reminding Minna to come to an understanding with von Seebach and work for the amnesty.

Page 166, *note* 1. That the interview was more serious than this description implies is proved by Wagner's own testimony in his letter to the Dresden lawyer Franz Adolf Schmidt on February 20, 1863, in which he earnestly pleads for von Beust's support in refuting the slander about his incendiarism.

Page 166, *note* 2. Von Beust's story does not inspire confidence, for several statements in it are notoriously false; for instance, the ridiculous remark about Wagner's share in the revolution, that the composer of *Rienzi* wanted to play the Tribune. The statement that Wagner was sentenced to death *in contumaciam* is incomprehensible, for von Beust must have known that no sentence was ever passed upon Wagner, since the prosecution was not proceeded with. Equally inaccurate is the statement that no demand was made for Wagner's extradition from Weimar, since von Beust had given satisfactory assurances. The fact is that Wagner could not go to Weimar, because King John himself flatly refused the Grand Duke's request.

Page 166, *note* 3. Müller takes von Beust's expression " no demonstrations " to mean the refusal of Wagner's thanks, whereas the interview with von Behr makes it quite plain that it refers to the fact that officials of the Ministry were afraid of demonstrations being made by Wagner's partisans when he appeared in public, and wished to avoid such occurrences.

Page 169, *note* 1. Privy Councillor Rudolf von Könneritz had long been Saxon Ambassador at Vienna, and had already shown hostility to Wagner in 1858–59, during his stay in Venice.

Page 172, *note* 1. We have already pointed out several times that these were really not the documents in Wagner's case, for there were none such, only a compilation of extracts from other documents, especially the examinations of other revolutionists, which concerned Wagner. There are several later entries relating to the attempts of the Ministry of Justice to collect fees of 50 thalers, 7 groschen, 5 pfennigs from Wagner. In 1864 the police reported that Wagner's lodgings were at No. 16

Walpurgisstrasse, on the first floor, but that he was not at home, and his wife was away for the summer; the servant-girl could only say that Wagner was still on his travels. When another attempt was made to collect the fees, on November 4, 1864, the court messenger reported that Frau Wagner stated that her husband was then at München. The Ministry does not seem ever to have got its money, for there is no record of the settlement of this claim.

Page 179, *note* 1. "Möser" is a reference to the Court music-dealer at Dresden, C. F. Meser, to whom Wagner had granted the right to sell the scores of his three early operas, *Rienzi, Der fliegende Holländer,* and *Tannhäuser,* on commission.

Page 181, *note* 1. This mutual aversion between Wagner and the other revolutionary refugees living at Zürich is confirmed not only by Wagner in various letters and by Köchly in the letter given here, but, with regard to Wagner's early stay at Zürich, by Carl Schurz. The refugees were not welcome visitors to the Swiss authorities, in spite of a certain sympathy with their republican views. Johann Ulrich Schiess, Chancellor of the Swiss Confederation, addressed a letter (Berne, October 19 and 23, 1849) to the Saxon Government. Switzerland, he says, had always assumed a correct attitude, and fulfilled all international obligations; he therefore hopes that the Saxon Government will agree to let the refugees in Switzerland return under amnesty. Switzerland cannot find them all employment, and their state of idleness gives rise to difficulties and political apprehensions, as their presence disturbs some of the cantons. On December 12, 1849, the Ministry of Justice replied that remission of penalties had already been made in the case of certain categories of the May rebels, but refused to grant a general amnesty to the refugees, because it would involve unequal treatment of them as compared with those who had remained in Saxony.

Page 181, *note* 2. Köchly writes in his letter to Schwender May 27, 1850:
"Among the people here, apart from Zschetzsche—we are now living at the Fröbel Institute—I meet Todt, Berthold, Zschweigert, and Hitzschold most often, and I see Tschirner sometimes. The blood-red republicans, such as Jäkel, Heerch, and Ludwig, cannot stand us, it seems. Their chief occupation is drinking!"

Page 182, *note* 1. Wagner also mentions Frau Klepperbein in his autobiography as "my motherly old friend." The firm of C. G. Klepperbein had an important druggist business in Dresden, which is still carried on in its old quarters at No. 9 Frauenstrasse.

Page 183, *note* 1. Dübner was seeing through the press the series of Greek authors published by the famous Paris house of Didot.

Page 186, *note* 1. Von Hülsen (born 1810, died 1886), a retired officer, became General Manager at Berlin in 1851.

Page 187, *note* 1. Dr Julius Hammer sent in his play *Die Brüder* to the Dresden Theatre, and had it back from Lüttichau for alteration. After making many changes and cuts, he handed it in again on October 26, 1855; on January 12, 1856, he thanks Pabst for its acceptance. The dress rehearsal was on March 29, and the first performance on March 30, but the piece ran for only three nights.

LIST OF PRINCIPAL
AUTHORITIES

ALTMANN, WILHELM. *Richard Wagners Briefe nach Zeitfolge und Inhalt* (Leipzig, 1905). (A collection of Wagner's letters arranged according to chronology and subject.)

CHAMBERLAIN, HOUSTON STEWART. *Richard Wagner* (Munich, 1896). English edition, translated by G. A. Hight (London, 1897).

ELLIS, WILLIAM ASHTON. 1849: *A Vindication* (Kegan Paul, 1892). (A historical retrospect in vindication of Wagner.) German edition, by Hans von Wolzogen (Leipzig).

GLASENAPP, CARL FRIEDRICH. *Das Leben Richard Wagners* (Leipzig).

KIETZ, GUSTAV ADOLPH. *Richard Wagner in den Jahren 1842–49 und 1873–75* (Dresden, 1905). (Recollections of G. A. Kietz, recorded by Marie Kietz.)

KOCH, MAX. *Richard Wagner* (Berlin, 1913 and 1918).

KUMMER, FRIEDRICH. "Dresdner Wagner-Annalen 1814-1913," in *Dresdner Richard-Wagner-Feier*. (Published in connexion with the centenary of Wagner's birth.)

MÜLLER, GEORG HERMANN. *Richard Wagner in der Mai-Revolution, 1849* (Dresden, 1919).

PRÖLSS, ROBERT. *Geschichte des Hoftheaters zu Dresden von seinen Anfängen bis zum Jahre 1862* (Dresden, 1878). (A history of the Dresden Court Theatre from its foundation to 1862.)

—— *Beiträge zur Geschichte des Hoftheaters zu Dresden in aktenmässiger Darstellung* (Erfurt). (Documents concerning the Dresden Court Theatre.)

RÖCKEL, AUGUST. *Sachsens Erhebung und das Zuchthaus zu Waldheim* (Frankfurt, 1865). (An account of the rising of 1849.)

SCHMIDT, LUDWIG. Documents relating to Wagner in *Zeitschrift der internationalen Musikgesellschaft*.

TILLE, ARMIN. "Grossherzog Karl Alexander und Richard Wagner," in *Deutsche Rundschau* (Berlin, 1925).

WAGNER, RICHARD. *Mein Leben.* Edited, with Introduction and Notes, by Wilhelm Altmann (Leipzig, 1911). English edition, *My Life* (Constable, 1911).
—— Collected writings, edited by Julius Kapp (14 vols., Leipzig, 1914).

CORRESPONDENCE

Richard Wagner an Minna Wagner (Berlin and Leipzig, 1908). English edition, *Richard to Minna Wagner,* translated by W. A. Ellis (London, 1909).

Briefwechsel zwischen Wagner und Liszt (Leipzig, 1908). English edition, *Correspondence of Wagner and Liszt,* translated by Francis Hueffer (London, 1888).

Richard Wagners Briefe an Theodor Uhlig, Wilhelm Fischer, Ferdinand Heine (Leipzig, 1888). English edition, *Richard Wagner's Letters to his Dresden Friends, Theodor Uhlig, Wilhelm Fischer, and Ferdinand Heine,* translated by J. S. Shedlock (London, 1890).

Richard Wagner an Mathilde Wesendonk. Edited, with an Introduction and Notes, by Wolfgang Golther (Leipzig, 1920). English edition, *Richard Wagner to Mathilde Wesendonck,* translated by W. A. Ellis (London, 1905). (Diaries and letters, 1853–71.)

Richard Wagners Briefe an Otto Wesendonk, 1852–70. Edited by Wolfgang Golther (Berlin, 1905).

Richard Wagners Briefe an Hans von Bülow (Jena, 1916).

Familienbriefe von Richard Wagner, 1832–74. Edited by Carl Friedrich Glasenapp (Berlin, 1907).

Richard Wagners Briefwechsel mit seinen Verlegern : vol. i, *Mit Breitkopf und Härtel,* edited by Wilhelm Altmann (Leipzig, 1912).

Richard Wagners Briefe an Frau Julie Ritter. Edited by Siegmund von Hausegger (Munich, 1920).

Richard Wagners Briefe an August Röckel. With Introduction by La Mara (Leipzig, 1894). English edition, *Richard Wagner's Letters to August Röckel,* translated by Eleanor C. Sellar (Bristol).

INDEX

O   209

INDEX

215

Coventry University

2